T0369642

exam✓success

in

FIRST LANGUAGE ENGLISH

for **Cambridge IGCSE**®

Oxford excellence for Cambridge IGCSE® & O Level

OXFORD
UNIVERSITY PRESS

OXFORD
UNIVERSITY PRESS

Great Clarendon Street, Oxford, OX2 6DP, United Kingdom

Oxford University Press is a department of the University of Oxford. It furthers the University's objective of excellence in research, scholarship, and education by publishing worldwide. Oxford is a registered trade mark of Oxford University Press in the UK and in certain other countries

© Jane Arredondo

The moral rights of the authors have been asserted

First published in 2019

British Library Cataloguing in Publication Data
Data available

978-0-19-844466-4

7 9 10 8 6

Paper used in the production of this book is a natural, recyclable product made from wood grown in sustainable forests.
The manufacturing process conforms to the environmental regulations of the country of origin.

Printed and bound by CPI Group (UK) Ltd, Croydon, CR0 4YY

Acknowledgements

The publisher and authors would like to thank the following for permission to use photographs and other copyright material:

Cover: Shutterstock

Artwork by Aptara Inc

We are grateful to the authors and publishers for use of extracts from their titles and in particular for the following:

Bill Bryson: Neither Here Nor There, Transworld Publishers. Copyright © Bill Bryson 1991. Reproduced by permission of the author and Penguin Random House Canada Limited.

Agatha Christie: The Thirteen Problems Copyright © 1932 by Agatha Christie Limited. Reprinted by permission of HarperCollins Publishers.

Angela Clarence: Adapted from 'A travel writer in the desert', The Observer, 21 May 2000. © Angela Clarence. Reproduced by permission of the author.

Sacha Dench: 'I loved every perilous and beautiful moment', www.pressreader.com © Good Housekeeping/Hearst Magazines UK. Reproduced by permission.

E M Forster: 'The Machine Stops' Copyright © E M Forster. The Provost and Scholars of King's College, Cambridge and the Society of Authors as the Literary Representatives of the E.M. Forster Estate.

Neil Gaiman: 201 words from 'Coraline' published October 2013, © Neil Gaiman 2002, Bloomsbury Publishing PLC. Reproduced by permission of Bloomsbury Publishing PLC and Writers House LLC acting as agent for the author/illustrator.

Brian Gallagher: 'An American in India', https://iaeste.org. Reproduced by permission.

Jean Gill: 'A Small Cheese in Provence'. Reproduced by permission of the author.

Susan Hill: Farthing House, Long Barn Books, Copyright © Susan Hill 2006. Reproduced by permission of Sheil Land Associates on behalf of the author.

Martin Hudson: 'Benefits far outweigh risk' from www. theguardian.com. Copyright Guardian News & Media Ltd 2018. Reproduced by permission.

Kazuo Ishiguro: Excerpt(s) from When We Were Orphans copyright © 2000 by Kazuo Ishiguro. Used by permission of Alfred A. Knopf, an imprint of the Knopf Doubleday Publishing Group, a division of Penguin Random House LLC and Faber and Faber Ltd. All rights reserved.

Eowyn Ivey: 'The Snow Child', Copyright © 2012 by Eowyn Ivey. Excerpts from 'The Snow Child' copyright © 1989 Freya Littledale. Reproduced by permission.

Alex Johnstone: Adapted from 'How a better understanding of the seven ages of appetite could help us stay healthy' from https:// theconversation.com. Reproduced by permission of the author.

Chloe Leighton: 'Horses: a Scythian's best friend' from https:// blog.britishmuseum.org. © The Trustees of the British Museum, 2018. Reproduced by permission.

Ann Mann & Hilary Rich: page 23 from Frankie Mae and Other Stories (Responses) published in 1987. Reproduced with permission of the Licensor through PLSclear.

Michelle A Miller & Francesco Cappuccio: Adapted from 'Why does the teenage brain need more sleep' https://theconversation. com. Reproduced by permission of the authors.

Ariane Rummery: 'Refugee education' from www.unhcr.org. Reproduced by permission of UNHCR and the author.

Although we have made every effort to trace and contact all copyright holders before publication this has not been possible in all cases. If notified, the publisher will rectify any errors or omissions at the earliest opportunity.

IGCSE® is the registered trademark of Cambridge Assessment International Education. All examination-style questions and answers within this publication have been written by the authors. In examination, the way marks are awarded may be different.

Contents

 Please go to www.oxfordsecondary.com/esg-for-caie-igcse for:
- Answers
- Glossary

Matched to the latest Cambridge assessment criteria, this in-depth Exam Success Guide brings clarity and focus to exam preparation with detailed and practical guidance on raising attainment in IGCSE® First Language English.

This Exam Success Guide:

- Is **fully matched** to the latest Cambridge IGCSE® & O Level syllabuses
- Includes comprehensive **recap** and **review** features which focus on key course content
- Equips you to **raise your grade** with sample responses and examiner commentary
- Will help you to **understand exam expectations** and avoid common mistakes with **examiner tips**
- **Apply knowledge** and test understanding via **exam-style questions**, with answers available online
- Is perfect for use alongside the *Complete First Language English for Cambridge IGCSE®* Student Book or as a standalone resource for independent revision

This Exam Success Guide has been carefully designed to maximise exam potential. The features which will help you:

- **Objectives** at the start of every section summarise key things you need to know for each topic.

- **Apply:** targeted revision activities are written specifically for these guides, which will help you to apply your knowledge in the exam paper. These provide a variety of transferrable exam skills and techniques. By using a variety of revision styles you'll be able to cement your revision.

- **Review:** throughout each section, you can review different aspects of the exam with these prompts.

- **Examiner comments:** strengthen exam performance through analysis of sample student answers and examiner responses.

- **Question Recap:** key information about the types of question you'll encounter in the exam, and what's expected of you.

- **Exam tips:** include particular emphasis on content and skills where students commonly struggle. The tips give details on how to maximise marks in the exam.

- **Link:** throughout the book, these include references back to the Student Book or link synoptically to other sections in your Exam Success Guide.

- **Raise your grade:** can be found at the end of each chapter. This section invites you to reflect on the examination skills you've gained and consolidates advice for assessment.

You will find the answers and glossary at www.oxfordsecondary.com/esg-for-caie-igcse

Introduction
Aiming for success

This exam success guide will help you to understand what is in the Cambridge IGCSE First Language English exam and to improve your key skills to achieve higher grades.

What is in this book

When you take your exam, you will sit Paper 1 Reading, which is compulsory.

You will also **either** sit Paper 2 Directed Writing and Composition **or** submit a Coursework Portfolio for Component 3. You may also take the optional Speaking and Listening Test, Component 4.

To help you prepare for the exam, this book:

- gives you all you need to know about each component
- helps you to understand what is required in different types of question
- helps you to improve your skills for each component to raise your grades
- gives you practice in answering exam-style questions.

Work through the units in order to help you become more familiar with the demands of each component and to achieve greater success in the exam. Use the Glossary to revise key terms. You can find the Glossary at www.oxfordsecondary.com/esg-for-caie-igcse,

You will improve the following skills:

Reading
- locating information and identifying specific details
- understanding a writer's intentions and choice of words and style
- making notes for a summary
- using and developing information for your own writing.

Writing
- writing a summary
- planning and organising your writing
- writing in different styles for discursive and persuasive compositions
- writing descriptive and narrative compositions.

Speaking and Listening
- preparing a short talk on a chosen topic
- participating in a two-way conversation about your topic.

The exam components

All Cambridge IGCSE First Language English candidates are examined in two components:

- Paper 1 – Reading, which is compulsory, **and**
- **either** Paper 2 – Directed Writing and Composition **or** Component 3 – Coursework Portfolio.

Candidates may also take Component 4 – Speaking and Listening Test, which is optional.

> The IGCSE First Language English exams ask you to show that you can:
> - read and understand a broad range of texts
> - understand how and why a text has been written
> - discuss a writer's choice of words and style
> - read critically, and use information and knowledge from your reading in your own writing
> - communicate clearly, accurately and effectively
> - use a wide range of vocabulary and appropriate grammar when you are writing and speaking
> - develop a personal style and change your style of writing for different audiences (readers and listeners) and different purposes (to inform, persuade or entertain).

Paper 1 – Reading

Time: 2 hours.

Worth: 80 marks, worth 50 per cent of your final grade.

Contents: Paper 1 contains three reading texts (A–C) and three compulsory questions. The three main questions contain sub-questions:

- **Question 1(a)–(e)** – short-answer questions on Text A to assess your comprehension and language skills
- **Question 1(f)** – a summary task on Text B
- **Question 2(a)–(c)** – short-answer questions on Text C to assess your language skills
- **Question 2(d)** – a longer language task on Text C about the writer's word choice and style
- **Question 3** – an extended writing task related to Text C.

 Link

You will find out more about these questions and the assessment objectives for Paper 1 in Unit 1.

Paper 2 – Directed Writing and Composition

Time: 2 hours.

Worth: 80 marks, worth 50 per cent of your final grade.

Contents: Paper 2 contains two sections:

- **Section A** is compulsory. You will be asked to read one or two texts, then answer a Directed Writing task in a specific style.
- **Section B** gives you a choice. It has four questions: two for descriptive compositions and two for narrative compositions. You choose one question and answer in the appropriate style.

 Link

You will find out more about these questions and the assessment objectives for Paper 2 in Unit 2.

Component 3 – Coursework Portfolio

Time: You complete your portfolio during your course, not in an exam.

Worth: 80 marks, worth 50 per cent of your final grade.

Contents: The Coursework Portfolio contains three different compositions. Each composition must be about 500–800 words. They may be completed in any order. They are:

- **Assignment 1** – writing to discuss, argue or persuade
- **Assignment 2** – writing to describe
- **Assignment 3** – writing to narrate.

 Link

You will find out more about these assignments and the assessment objectives for Component 3 in Unit 3.

Component 4 – Speaking and Listening Test

Contents: The Speaking and Listening Test is in two parts:

- **Part 1** – you give a short talk for 3–4 minutes on a topic of your choice
- **Part 2** – you engage in conversation for 7–8 minutes with your teacher and/or examiner about your topic.

The whole test is recorded and lasts approximately 10–12 minutes. It is not compulsory and marks are *separate* to Components 1–3.

 Link

You will find out more about this test and the assessment objectives for Component 4 in Unit 4.

Command words

The questions and tasks in Papers 1 and 2 use command words in very specific ways. Study the command words on page 25 of the syllabus, to be found at www.cambridgeinternational.org/igcse. Think about what they are asking you to do.

Assessment objectives and marking guidelines

You will find the assessment objectives (AOs) for the exam questions and tasks in the relevant parts of Units 1–4. You will also find the marking guidelines at the back of this book. These offer level descriptions, rather than set or specific answers, because answers will vary according to the specific texts. You can use the level descriptions as a guide to your progress.

 You will find the answers at http://www.oxfordsecondary.com/esg-for-caie-igcse

 **Review**

Before continuing, assess your own aims and the progress you have made so far by answering the questions on the next few pages. You can return to them as you work through the book to revise your answers if you wish and to see how well you are preparing for the exam.

1 **My target grade:** ....
2 **How taking Cambridge IGCSE First Language English will help me in the future:**
   - Reading skills ....
   ....

- Writing skills ....

  ....

- Speaking skills ....

  ....

- Listening skills ....

  ....

- Further education and other subjects ....

  ....

- Getting a job ....

  ....

- Being successful in my chosen career ....

  ....

- Other ways ....

  ....

3   My motivation to do well in the exam (1 is very poor, 5 is very strong). Tick where you are on the scale.

1 ⟶ 2 ⟶ 3 ⟶ 4 ⟶ 5

4   My strengths and weaknesses in reading

	Always	I need more practice
I enjoy reading for pleasure.		
I have a wide vocabulary.		
I am not put off by new vocabulary or words that are long or difficult to pronounce.		
I can make sense of a piece of writing when I encounter difficult or new words.		
I can understand the content of newspapers and magazine articles.		
I can recognise the writing style for:		
• fiction		
• non-fiction		
• news report		
• news article		
• informative		
• narrative		
• discursive		
• persuasive		
• descriptive.		

5 My strengths and weaknesses in writing

	Always	I need more practice
I can write in the appropriate style for:		
• narrative fiction for short stories		
• script or radio transcripts		
• news reports		
• blog and news articles		
• informative texts		
• discursive texts		
• persuasive texts		
• descriptive texts to inform and entertain.		

6 My strengths and weaknesses in speaking and listening

	Always	I need more practice
I feel confident when I give a speech or a talk to an audience on a subject of my choice.		
I can use a wide range of vocabulary to express my thoughts, ideas and feelings.		
I can explain details well.		
I know when to adapt/change my use of language for different purposes.		
I can modify/change my tone for different listeners.		
I can answer questions appropriately without going off the topic.		
I am not afraid of expressing my opinions.		
I enjoy participating in conversations.		
I can identify a speaker's tone of voice.		
I can identify a speaker's implicit meaning.		

Exam tip

Here are some ways to improve your speaking skills:

- listen to radio documentaries
- listen to TED talks
- watch television documentaries
- watch and listen to news programmes
- practise with friends.

What other ways can you use to improve?

 Link

You can find information on all the writing styles referred to above in the *Complete First Language English for Cambridge IGCSE® Student Book.*

Objectives

In this unit you will:

- Explore what is in Paper 1
- Practise keywording questions and annotating texts
- Practise answering the different types of question
- Compare your answers with sample answers and examiner comments
- Review your progress and how to raise your grade

Review

Paper 1 Reading is compulsory

All students take Paper 1. This part of the Cambridge IGCSE First Language English exam is where you show how well you can read, understand and interpret different types of text.

During your course, you have developed your reading skills by reading a range of texts from the 20th and 21st centuries. This has included literature, fiction and non-fiction, news reports and articles. Now you are being asked to show how well you understand what you read and how writers use language to achieve certain effects.

This unit will help you to understand the different types of question in Paper 1, the assessment objectives and what examiners are looking for in your answers. Work through the unit, then answer the review questions at the end to monitor your progress.

Preparing for Paper 1 involves improving your reading skills so that you are more effective at:

- keywording questions
- skimming and scanning texts to find information
- annotating texts
- writing a summary
- discussing the writer's craft.

What is in Paper 1

Paper 1 includes three compulsory questions and three texts (A–C), printed in a separate insert. Together, Texts A and B will be 700–750 words in length. Text C will be 500–650 words in length.

Spend at least 15 minutes reading the texts *before* you start reading the question paper. You will not have a dictionary so if you encounter new or difficult words, spend some time making sure you can follow the meaning. When you are happy that you have understood the content of the texts, read and keyword the questions carefully.

Question 1

The whole of this question is worth 30 marks. It is divided into a Comprehension task (Question 1(a)–(e)) and a Summary task (Question 1(f)). You will be asked to read Text A and Text B, printed on a separate exam paper insert.

Comprehension task – Question 1(a)–(e)

These are short-answer questions on Text A. They test your reading comprehension and how well you understand words and phrases.

The questions will include the command words "give", "identify" and "describe". You will also be asked to "explain" details in your own words. This means you must rephrase the writer's words and not copy from the text.

Exam tip

Organising your time for Paper 1

You have two hours for Paper 1 and have to answer three questions. The marks for each question or sub-question will give you some indication of how much time you should spend on each one. Keep checking your watch to make sure you don't spend too much time on each question, but don't avoid re-reading the texts.

Assessment objectives

Question 1(a)–(e) tests your reading skills
You will be asked to:

- show you understand explicit meanings in the text
- show you understand implicit meanings and attitudes
- select details and use information in your own words.

Summary task – Question 1(f)

This question requires you to respond to Text B by writing a selective summary to show how well you:

- understand Text B, using your reading skills
- can select and use information in your writing.

You will need to write a summary of no more than 120 words in continuous writing. There are 15 marks for Question 1(f): 10 marks for reading and 5 marks for writing.

Assessment objectives

Question 1(f) tests your reading skills
You need to show how well you:

- understand explicit meanings in the text
- understand implicit meanings and attitudes
- select details and use information in your own words.

Question 1(f) also tests your summary writing skills
You need to show how well you:

- organise ideas and structure your writing according to the task
- use appropriate vocabulary, different sentence structures and style.

Question 2

For this question, you need to read Text C. The question is divided into short-answer questions (Question 2(a)–(c)) and a Language task (Question 2(d)). The short-answer questions are worth a total of 10 marks and the Language task is worth 15 marks.

For the Language task, you need to respond to Text C by writing about 200–300 words on how the writer has achieved certain effects and influenced the reader. This means you need to be able to identify linguistic devices and/or literary features and discuss the writer's style.

Assessment objectives

Question 2 tests how well you understand the writer's craft
You need to show that you understand:

- explicit meanings (what the writer is saying)
- implicit meanings and attitudes (what is suggested or implied)
- how writers use language to achieve effects and influence readers.

Question 3

This question asks for an extended response to Text C. It is worth 25 marks: 15 marks are for the reading assessment objectives and 10 marks for the writing assessment objectives. You will be asked to write about 250–350 words using one of the following text types: letter, report, journal, speech, interview or article.

Assessment objectives

Question 3 tests reading and writing skills
You need to show how well you can:

- understand explicit meanings
- understand implicit meanings and attitudes

Link

Prepare for the Language task by studying the Glossary at www.oxfordsecondary.com/esg-for-caie-igcse and reviewing your work on the writer's craft in the *Complete First Language English for Cambridge IGCSE® Student Book*. If you are also taking IGCSE English Literature, use your literary analysis skills.

- analyse, evaluate and develop facts, ideas and opinions in the text using relevant examples from Text C to support your views.

Your writing should demonstrate that you can:

- articulate and clearly express what you think, feel and imagine
- organise and structure paragraphs for a deliberate effect or purpose
- use vocabulary and different sentence structures according to the context
- use register appropriate to the context.

 QuestionRecap

Take about 15 minutes to read the three texts, before you turn to the questions.

Exam tip

You can annotate the texts and use any space for planning, but don't write your answers on the insert.

Sample Paper 1

 Apply

1 Read the sample paper on the following pages. Read the texts first, then the questions.

2 Explore how Question 1(a)–(e) has been keyworded and how Text A has been annotated by another student on pages 22–3.

3 Return to the sample paper and answer Question 1(a)–(e) in the spaces provided.

4 Compare your answers with those of a successful student on pages 22–3.

📖 Text A: Silence

This text is about different types of silence.

According to the poet Philip Gross, writing in the Spring issue of *The Author*, when one says the word "silence" it "feels like noise". He then goes on to list "a whole crowd of meanings" related to "silence". There is, he says, "Angry silence, a Victorian parent's children-should-be-seen-and-not-heard silence. Worse, the bad silence of secrets in the family." There is the

5 "silencing" of censorship. But there is also the joy of silence, such as when a poet can feel an audience's "deep listening".

Most of us have ambivalent attitudes to silence. On the one hand, it is desirable – we need it to be creative or to focus clearly on a task in hand like writing or revision – but in other ways, it is to be feared. There's that awful moment after you tell someone something

10 and there's no response: a joke that's met with silence or the unspoken words of terrible fear. There's the you-could-hear-a-pin-drop anticipation of an audience waiting for a performance to begin and the deathly, unwelcome silence when there's no applause. There's the gift of silence as you see a glorious view for the first time and hear yourself sigh; there's the appalling silence when you realise everyone is staring at you.

15 Gross goes on to say that most writers "can only breathe and write in silence", but many writers can work well amid the bustle and hubbub of cafés. J.K. Rowling wrote most of her first Harry Potter story in a café, so that's testament to that.

Then there is the conundrum of caring for babies: most parents are afraid a sudden din might wake a sleeping infant, yet one of the best ways to soothe a fretful baby is to place it near a

20 loaded washing machine – apparently rumbling white noise reminds them of the womb.

So, much as I love the absence of commotion in any form, I have to accept that silence perhaps isn't natural for other human beings.

Text B: Noise pollution

This text is about noise pollution.

Noise pollution is undesirable or disruptive sound that interferes with normal daily activity for humans and wildlife. Inappropriate noise can disrupt our sleep and conversation, and diminish our quality of life. It is now also shown to have a profound effect on nature and
5   our environment.

Noise pollution is generated in numerous ways, including road, air and sea transport, construction machinery, and even domestic machinery such as lawn mowers. Excessive, unnecessary human noise includes loud music in shops, shouting in the street, the compulsive
10   communicator on a phone … This is human disturbance affecting humans, but now studies are revealing how noise pollution is also causing harmful effects to plants, animals, trees and marine life.

According to the World Health Organisation, excessive noise "seriously harms human health and interferes with people's daily activities". We
15   know it disturbs sleep, but it can also damage hearing and mental health to such an extent that it can cause heart attacks and changes in social behaviour. The eco website, Everything Connects, recently outlined how excessive noise is affecting the *areas* in which we live: "Human noise can have ripple effects on long-lived plants and trees that can last for
20   decades even after the sources of noise subside. Many plants and trees rely on birds and other animals to deliver pollen from one flower or tree to the next, or to disperse their seeds, but many animals are adapting to the noise by changing their behaviour or moving to quieter locales. Consequently, noise pollution is altering the landscape of plants and
25   trees, which depend on noise-affected animals to pollinate them and spread their seeds."

Noise in rural areas, and even in gardens, can alter the fine balance of nature. Most predators need a "natural silence" to detect their prey. Loud human chatter on a country walk might be short-lived, but when
30   noise is long term the creatures that use sound to hunt can go hungry and, worse, fail to feed their young. Constant loud noise is causing species such as bats and owls to abandon their habitats. Garden birds have to sing at stressful higher frequencies to attract their mates. Noise generated by ships' engines can disturb sea mammals' signals and even
35   cause them to stray from migration routes, with knock-on effects such as the decline in numbers of whales and dolphins. Excessive human and traffic noise in rural areas, on the coast and at sea is reducing usable habitat, which in the case of endangered species may be a short cut to extinction.

Text C: An unpleasant welcome

This text is taken from the memoir A Moment of War *by the English author and poet Laurie Lee. As a young man Lee crossed the Pyrenees from France into Spain, arriving in December 1937 to participate in the Spanish Civil War. Coming down from the mountains, Lee finds his way to a poor dwelling where he is given a strange welcome. The next day he is put in a cart. He thinks he is going to join the Republicans.*

There was a motionless silence while they took me in – seeing a young tattered stranger, coatless and soaked to the knees, carrying a kit-bag from which a violin bow protruded. Suddenly the old woman said "Ay!" and beckoned me to the fire, which was piled high with glowing pine cones. I crouched, thawing out by the choking fumes, sensing deeply

5 this moment of arrival. […]

[The next morning] the boys half-marched me into the lane and the rest of the family followed and stood watching, blowing on their purple fingers. […] The cart waiting in the lane resembled a rough-looking tumbril, and the driver had a cavernous, nervous face. "*Vamanos, vamanos, vamanos,*" he kept muttering plaintively, giving me glances of sharp

10 distaste. The boys helped me into the back of the cart and climbed up after me.

"Here he is. The English one," they said with ponderous jocularity. The driver sniffed, and uncoiled his whip.

"Horse and cart," said one of the brothers, nudging me smartly. "We've got to save your legs. They must be half destroyed with all this walking over mountains. And what

15 have we got if we haven't got your legs? You wouldn't be much use to us, would you?"

I was beginning to get a bit bored with all this levity, and sat there silent and shivering. The boys perched close beside me, one on each side, holding their guns at the ready, like sentries. Every so often they pointed them at me and nodded brightly. They appeared to be in a state of nervous high spirits.

20 "*Vamanos!*" snarled the driver and shook up the reins crossly. The old man and his wife raised their hands solemnly and told me to go with God. The little girl threw a stone at the horse, or it may have been at me, but it hit the horse and caused it to start with a jerk. So we began to lumber and creak down the steep rocky lane, the brothers now holding me by either elbow. The Pyrenees stood high behind us, white and hard, their peaks colouring to

25 the rising sun. The boys nodded towards them, grinning, nudging me sharply again, and baring their chestnut-tinted teeth.

Through the iced winter morning, slipping over glassy rocks, we made our stumbling way down the valley, passing snow-covered villages, empty and bare, from which all life and sound seemed withdrawn. This chilling silence was surely not one of nature, which

30 could be broken by a goat-bell or the chirp of a bird. It was as if a paralysing pestilence had visited the place, and I was to notice it on a number of occasions in the weeks to come. It was simply the stupefying numbness of war.

After an hour or so we came to a small hill town still shuttered by the shadow of rocks. A bent woman crept by, bearing a great load of firewood. A cat shot through a hole in a wall.

35 I noticed that the brothers had suddenly grown tense and anxious, sitting straight as pillars, thin-lipped, beside me. Two militiamen, in khaki ponchos, came out of a doorway and marched ahead of us down the street. Even our driver perked up and began to look around

him with what appeared to be an air of importance.
The militiamen led us into the square, to the
40 dilapidated Town Hall, from which the Republican
flag was hanging. The brothers called out to a couple
of sentries who were sitting on the steps, and one
of them got up and went inside. Now for a proper
welcome, I thought. I got down from the cart, and the
45 brothers followed. Then four soldiers came out with
fixed bayonets.

"We've brought you the spy," said the brothers,
and pushed me forward. The soldiers closed round
me and handcuffed my wrists.

From *A Moment of War* by Laurie Lee

 QuestionRecap

You have 2 hours to answer all
the questions.

Exam tip

Write your answers in the
spaces provided. If you need
more space, use extra sheets
of paper, numbering your
answers clearly.

 Activity

Read **Text A, *Silence***, and then answer **Question 1(a)–(e).**

Question 1

(a) Give **two** examples of "bad silence", according to the text.

- ....

- ....

[2]

(b) Using your own words, explain what the writer means by:

(i) A Victorian parent's "children-should-be-seen-and-not-heard silence" (lines 3–4)

....

....

[2]

(ii) the "silencing" of censorship (lines 4–5)

....

....

[2]

(c) Re-read paragraph 2 ("Most of us … everyone is staring at you.")
Give **two** reasons why actors and musicians might like and dislike silence (one reason
for like and one for dislike).

- ....

- ....

[2]

(d) Re-read paragraphs 3, 4 and 5 ("Gross goes on to say … silence perhaps isn't natural for other human beings.")

    (i) Identify **one** example of an author who works well amid the "bustle" of a café, according to the text.

      ....

                                                                         [1]

    (ii) Explain why parents of small children might be confused about the need for silence at bedtime according to the text.

      ....

      ....

      ....

                                                                         [3]

(e) Re-read the whole text.

    Using your own words, explain why most people have "ambivalent attitudes" to silence, according to the text.

    ....

    ....

    ....

                                                                         [3]

Read **Text B, *Noise pollution***, and then answer **Question 1(f).**

Question 1

(f) According to **Text B**, how can noise pollution affect the environment, wildlife and aquatic mammals?

    You must **use continuous writing** (not note form) and **use your own words** as much as possible. Your summary should be no more than 120 words.
    Up to 10 marks are available for the content of your writing and up to 5 marks for the quality of your writing.

    ....

    ....

    ....

    ....

    ....

    ....

    ....

    ....

    ....

    ....

....

....

....

....

....

....

....

....

....

[15]

(If you need more lines, write on an extra sheet of paper. Remember to write your name and the question number at the top.)

Read **Text C, *An unpleasant welcome***, and then answer **Question 2(a)–(d).**

Question 2

Answer all the questions, **Question 2(a)–(d)**

(a) Identify a word or phrase from the text that suggests the same idea as the <u>words underlined</u>.

(i) The boys with Lee appeared to be in a state of <u>over-excited good humour</u>.

....

[1]

(ii) The driver gave Lee <u>quick looks of unpleasant dislike</u>.

....

[1]

(iii) Lee was taken to the Town Hall, which looked <u>in a state of disrepair</u>.

....

[1]

(iv) They passed through snow-covered <u>silent and abandoned villages</u>.

....

[1]

(b) Using your own words, explain what the writer means by each of the words underlined:

I was beginning to get a bit bored with all this <u>levity</u>, and sat there silent and shivering. The boys <u>perched</u> close beside me, one on each side, holding their guns at the ready, like <u>sentries</u>. Every so often they pointed them at me and nodded brightly. They appeared to be in a state of nervous high spirits.

(i) levity   .... **[1]**

(ii) perched .... **[1]**

(iii) sentries .... **[1]**

(c) Use **one** example of a word or phrase from the text below to explain how the writer suggests he is going to have a much harder time in Spain than he had expected. **Use your own words in your explanation**.

Through the iced winter morning, slipping over glassy rocks, we made our stumbling way down the valley, passing snow-covered villages, empty and bare, from which all life and sound seemed withdrawn. This chilling silence was surely not one of nature, which could be broken by a goat-bell or the chirp of a bird. It was as if a paralysing pestilence had visited the place, and I was to notice it on a number of occasions in the weeks to come.

....

....

....

....

....

....

[3]

(d) Re-read paragraphs 7 and 8.

- Paragraph 7 begins "Through the iced winter morning ..." and tells of Lee's journey on the cart.
- Paragraph 8 begins "After an hour or so ..." and is about arriving in a small hill town.

Explain how the writer uses language to convey meaning and to create effect in these paragraphs. Choose **three** examples of words or phrases from **each** paragraph to support your answer. Your choices should include the use of imagery. Write about 200–300 words.

Up to 15 marks are available for the content of your answer.

....

....

....

....

....

....

....

....

....

....

....

....

....

....

....

....

....

....

....

....

....

....

....

[15]

(If you need more lines, write on an extra sheet of paper. Remember to write your name and the question number at the top.)

Re-read **Text C, *An unpleasant welcome***, and then answer **Question 3.**

Question 3

Imagine you are one of the Spanish boys on the cart. Some years later you are interviewed about your memories of Laurie Lee and the Civil War for a radio programme. The interviewer asks you the following questions only:

- What did you see **and** feel during your journey with Laurie Lee to the town?
- What do you remember of his behaviour **and** reactions that day?
- What were your reasons for thinking he was a spy **and** what did you feel about seeing him in handcuffs?

Write the words of the interview.

Base your interview on what you have read in **Text C**, but be careful to use your own words. Address each of the three bullet points.

Begin your interview with the first question.

Write about 250–350 words.

Up to 15 marks are available for the content of your answer and up to 10 marks for the quality of your writing.

....

....

....

....

....

....

....

....

....

....

....

....

....

....

....

....

....

....

....

....

....

....

....

....

....

....

....

....

[25]

(If you need more lines, write on an extra sheet of paper. Remember to write your name and the question number at the top.)

Keywording questions

It is important to keyword (or annotate) each question in order to find the root of the question and be sure how to answer it. Look on page 22 at how a successful student keyworded Question 1(a)–(e).

The command words in these short-answer questions tell you what to do, but you also need to keyword other parts of each sub-question to decide exactly what is being asked. Take your time to read each question, then use a pencil or coloured pencils to underline (or circle) key words and write notes.

Some of these questions may have alternative answers, but all the alternatives must be in the text. You will be asked to explain explicit and implicit meanings, but you must identify and infer only what is in the text.

> **Exam tip**
>
> **Keywording questions**
> Always underline or circle the key words. Avoid using highlighters because if you make a mistake you can't erase it and you may forget it was wrong.

Keywording and answering Question 1(a)–(e)

📖 **Activity**

Read **Text A, *Silence*,** and then answer **Question 1(a)–(e)**.

In the text – not my own opinion or ideas

Question 1

Keyword = give = find details in the text

(a) Give **two** examples of "bad silence", according to the text.

Only 2

• When a joke is met with silence not laughter
• When an audience doesn't clap after a concert or play

[2]

Don't quote, show I understand what the writer is saying

Keyword = explain = show how I understand

(b) Using your own words, explain what the writer means by:

Explain what this means = Victorians were strict parents

(i) A Victorian parent's "children-should-be-seen-and-not-heard silence" (line 3)

When a very strict parent stops children from talking or behaving in a normal way

[2]

(ii) the "silencing" of censorship (line 5)

When people are prevented from speaking freely

[2]

Look at the sentence these words are in and use the same context

Keyword = give; use my own reasoning

(c) Re-read paragraph 2 ("Most of us … everyone is staring at you."). Give **two** reasons why actors and musicians might like and dislike silence (one reason for like and one for dislike).

Only actors and musicians

Opposites

• It shows the audience are listening.
• It also shows they do not like what they hear or see.

[2]

Only 1 for each

(d) Re-read paragraphs 3, 4 and 5 ("Gross goes on to say … silence perhaps isn't natural for other human beings.").

Only 1

Keyword = identify = find a detail or piece of information

(i) Identify **one** example of an author who works well amid the "bustle" of a café, according to the text.

J.K Rowling

[1]

A writer who can work in noisy surroundings

Keyword = explain; use the text – ideas and my interpretation of what has been written. Justify views??

(ii) Explain why parents of small children might be confused about the need for silence at bedtime, according to the text.

Parents think babies need silence to sleep or stay asleep because they (the parents) do but research shows babies sleep in noise and a gentle rhythm is like the sounds in the womb.

[3]

What parents normally assume and evidence they might be wrong

Keyword = explain

(e) Re-read the whole text.

Using your own words, explain why most people have "ambivalent attitudes" to silence, according to the text.

Don't lift or copy text

People both like and dislike silence. Sometimes it can be peaceful and help you to work, but it can also mean disapproval of a joke or your beliefs, as in censorship, and people do not like this.

[3]

Ambivalent = two opposing views or mixed feelings

Stick to what is in Text A, just enough for 3 marks

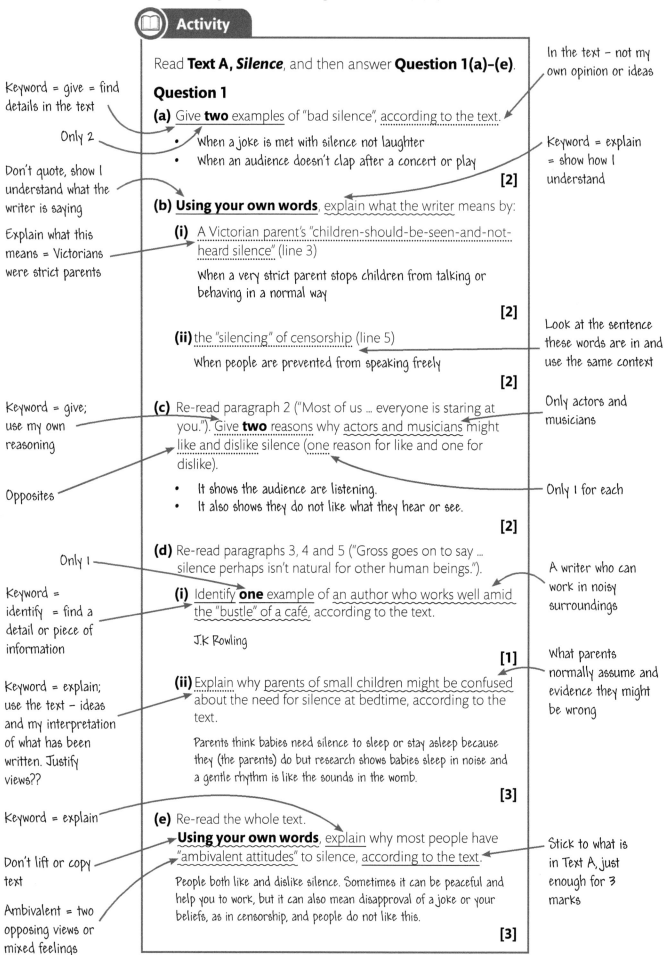

Skimming, scanning and annotating texts

To find the information in the texts and answer the questions, you need to use your skimming and scanning skills, and annotate the text.

Look below at how the student used the text to find answers for Question 1(a)–(e).

There are various options for Question 1(a), but you are only asked for two. This student chose not to repeat 'the silencing of "censorship"' for Question 1(a) because it forms part of Question 1(b). In this way, the student shows understanding of the text and the vocabulary.

Question 1(c) asks for two reasons: only one for like and one for dislike. You need to show you understand what is implied by "you-could-hear-a-pin-drop" in this context and the use of the word "deathly".

Question 1(d) wants you to find the word "bustle" and explain who can write in the "hubbub" of a noisy place.

Annotating Text A

Text A: Silence

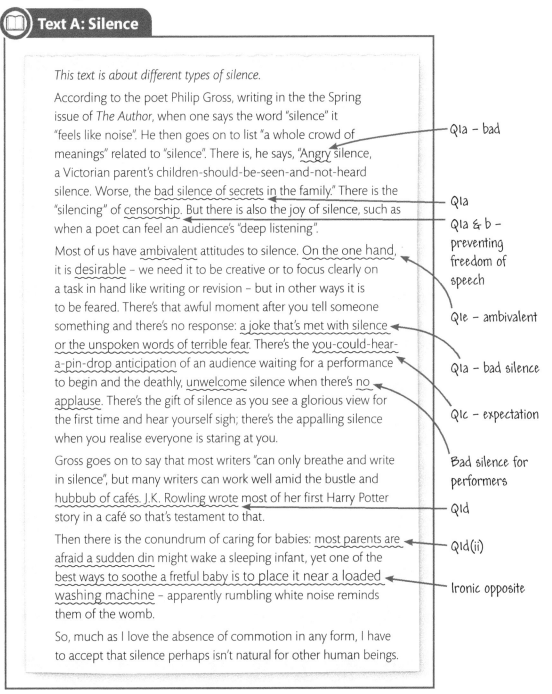

This text is about different types of silence.

According to the poet Philip Gross, writing in the the Spring issue of *The Author*, when one says the word "silence" it "feels like noise". He then goes on to list "a whole crowd of meanings" related to "silence". There is, he says, "Angry silence, a Victorian parent's children-should-be-seen-and-not-heard silence. Worse, the bad silence of secrets in the family." There is the "silencing" of censorship. But there is also the joy of silence, such as when a poet can feel an audience's "deep listening".

Q1a – bad

Q1a

Q1a & b – preventing freedom of speech

Most of us have ambivalent attitudes to silence. On the one hand, it is desirable – we need it to be creative or to focus clearly on a task in hand like writing or revision – but in other ways it is to be feared. There's that awful moment after you tell someone something and there's no response: a joke that's met with silence or the unspoken words of terrible fear. There's the you-could-hear-a-pin-drop anticipation of an audience waiting for a performance to begin and the deathly, unwelcome silence when there's no applause. There's the gift of silence as you see a glorious view for the first time and hear yourself sigh; there's the appalling silence when you realise everyone is staring at you.

Q1e – ambivalent

Q1a – bad silence

Q1c – expectation

Bad silence for performers

Gross goes on to say that most writers "can only breathe and write in silence", but many writers can work well amid the bustle and hubbub of cafés. J.K. Rowling wrote most of her first Harry Potter story in a café so that's testament to that.

Q1d

Then there is the conundrum of caring for babies: most parents are afraid a sudden din might wake a sleeping infant, yet one of the best ways to soothe a fretful baby is to place it near a loaded washing machine – apparently rumbling white noise reminds them of the womb.

Q1d(ii)

Ironic opposite

So, much as I love the absence of commotion in any form, I have to accept that silence perhaps isn't natural for other human beings.

Link

There is more advice on skimming and scanning on page 108 of this book and in "Reading to identify information" on page 6 of the *Complete First Language English for Cambridge IGCSE®* Student Book.

Link

You will find more advice on writing a selective summary on page 114.

Answering Question 1(f)

This is a selective summary task. First look at how a successful student keyworded this question and annotated Text B.

Keywording Question 1(f) and annotating Text B

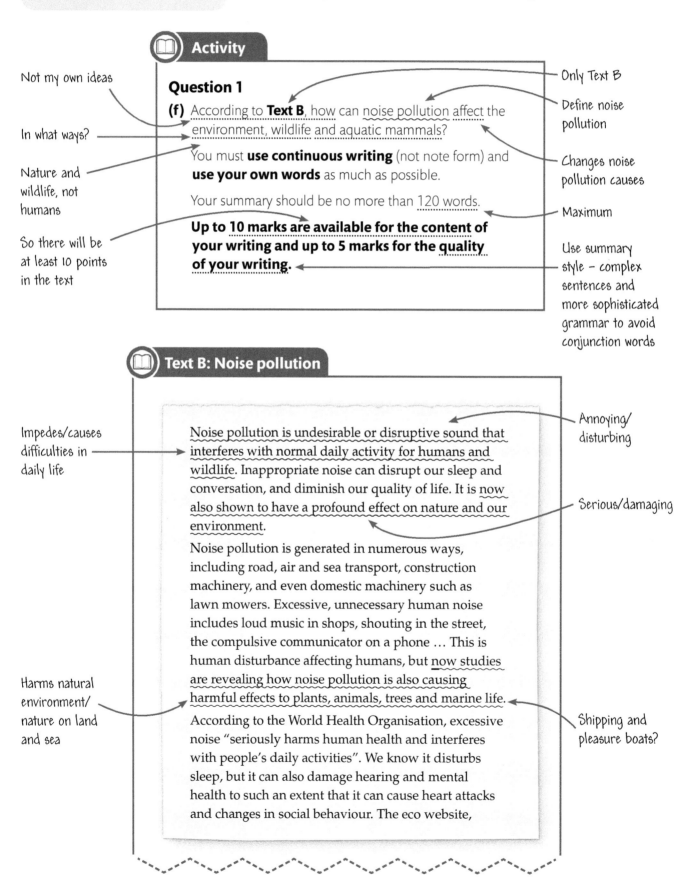

Not my own ideas

In what ways?

Nature and wildlife, not humans

So there will be at least 10 points in the text

Activity

Question 1

(f) According to **Text B**, how can noise pollution affect the environment, wildlife and aquatic mammals?

You must **use continuous writing** (not note form) and **use your own words** as much as possible.

Your summary should be no more than 120 words.

Up to 10 marks are available for the content of your writing and up to 5 marks for the quality of your writing.

Only Text B

Define noise pollution

Changes noise pollution causes

Maximum

Use summary style – complex sentences and more sophisticated grammar to avoid conjunction words

Text B: Noise pollution

Impedes/causes difficulties in daily life

Noise pollution is undesirable or disruptive sound that interferes with normal daily activity for humans and wildlife. Inappropriate noise can disrupt our sleep and conversation, and diminish our quality of life. It is now also shown to have a profound effect on nature and our environment.

Noise pollution is generated in numerous ways, including road, air and sea transport, construction machinery, and even domestic machinery such as lawn mowers. Excessive, unnecessary human noise includes loud music in shops, shouting in the street, the compulsive communicator on a phone … This is human disturbance affecting humans, but now studies are revealing how noise pollution is also causing harmful effects to plants, animals, trees and marine life.

Harms natural environment/ nature on land and sea

According to the World Health Organisation, excessive noise "seriously harms human health and interferes with people's daily activities". We know it disturbs sleep, but it can also damage hearing and mental health to such an extent that it can cause heart attacks and changes in social behaviour. The eco website,

Annoying/ disturbing

Serious/damaging

Shipping and pleasure boats?

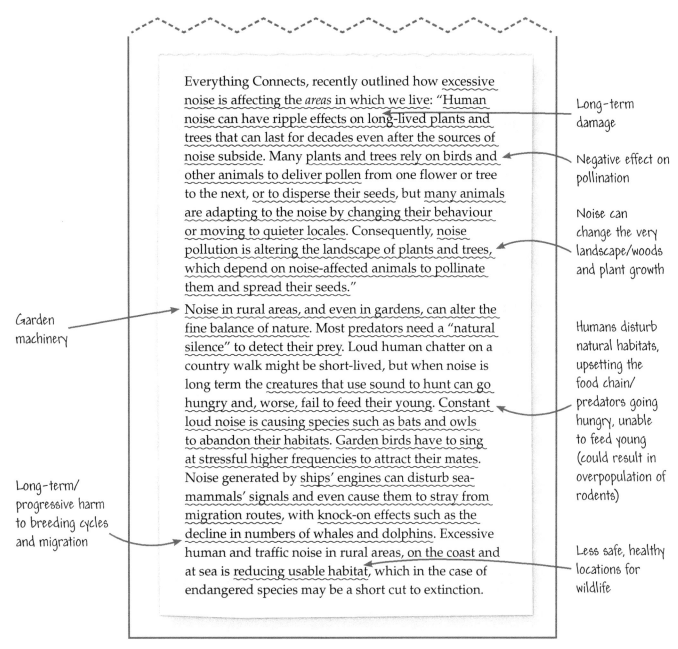

Long-term damage

Negative effect on pollination

Noise can change the very landscape/woods and plant growth

Garden machinery

Humans disturb natural habitats, upsetting the food chain/ predators going hungry, unable to feed young (could result in overpopulation of rodents)

Long-term/ progressive harm to breeding cycles and migration

Less safe, healthy locations for wildlife

Text within the annotated passage:

Everything Connects, recently outlined how excessive noise is affecting the *areas* in which we live: "Human noise can have ripple effects on long-lived plants and trees that can last for decades even after the sources of noise subside. Many plants and trees rely on birds and other animals to deliver pollen from one flower or tree to the next, or to disperse their seeds, but many animals are adapting to the noise by changing their behaviour or moving to quieter locales. Consequently, noise pollution is altering the landscape of plants and trees, which depend on noise-affected animals to pollinate them and spread their seeds."

Noise in rural areas, and even in gardens, can alter the fine balance of nature. Most predators need a "natural silence" to detect their prey. Loud human chatter on a country walk might be short-lived, but when noise is long term the creatures that use sound to hunt can go hungry and, worse, fail to feed their young. Constant loud noise is causing species such as bats and owls to abandon their habitats. Garden birds have to sing at stressful higher frequencies to attract their mates. Noise generated by ships' engines can disturb sea-mammals' signals and even cause them to stray from migration routes, with knock-on effects such as the decline in numbers of whales and dolphins. Excessive human and traffic noise in rural areas, on the coast and at sea is reducing usable habitat, which in the case of endangered species may be a short cut to extinction.

Writing a summary for Question 1(f)

The best way to understand what is required for Question 1(f) is to do it yourself.

Apply

1 Re-read Text B on page 13.
2 Re-read and keyword Question 1(f) on page 16, so you understand exactly what you are being asked to do. This is a *selective* summary task so you will not need to summarise the entire text, just the part identified in the question.
3 Identify and annotate parts of the text to select relevant details.
4 Number the details in the margin so you have at least ten points.
5 Rewrite the points in note form, using your own words and ticking off each point to make sure you have included everything.
6 Rewrite the notes, linking the details and writing them out as clearly and concisely as you can.
7 Check the word count and **do not** write more than 120 words. You should have at least 115 words to make sure you have included all the relevant points. If necessary, edit your summary. Write the number of words at the end of the summary.

> **Exam tip**
>
> **Check everything carefully**
> - Re-read the question and check you have answered it.
> - Check you have included all the relevant details in your summary.
> - Proofread your summary and make any necessary corrections.
> - Write the right amount. If you have fewer than 115 words, you have probably left something out. If you have more than 120 words, your summary may be in an inappropriate style.

Sample answer 1(f) and examiner comments

Now study a successful student's answer to Question 1(f) and examiner comments on the answer. You will see that the student has crossed through some sections to keep to the correct word count and the examiner has highlighted appropriate points.

 Activity

Question 1

(f) Noise pollution in the natural environment is loud, unnatural sound caused by people and ~~man-made~~ machines. This disturbs quiet locations where birds and mammals seek food and shelter. ~~Loud noise in gardens and fields also has a negative effect on wildlife.~~ Research now shows plants are also suffering, due to the changes in animal behaviour. Predators cannot hunt in silence so there can be an over-population of rodents; birds are prevented from finding food for their young, causing them to die. ~~This in turn causes Noise~~ Garden and farm machinery is causing a long-term imbalance in the food chain and affecting pollination and affecting plant growth. At sea, ships' engines are affecting how sea-mammals communicate and ~~instinctive~~ migrate. The reduction in safe ~~natural~~ habitat for birds and mammals on land and at sea is putting endangered species at great risk. (118 words)

Annotations:
- Developed
- Correct use of punctuation
- Uses the text in own words
- Developed idea
- Shows thorough understanding of text & good use of language
- Has cut summary to meet the word count effectively

 Examiner comments

Reading: 10/10 marks

An effective response, demonstrating thorough understanding of the text and the task. It develops text to show understanding of relevant ideas and is consistently well-focused. Points are skilfully selected to demonstrate an overview.

Writing: 4/5 marks

A relevant response, expressed clearly and fluently. It is mostly concise (it needed cutting to meet the word limit, suggesting there was no first draft). It is well organised and has a sound structure leading to the final sentence. The student uses their own words and rephrases the text well where necessary, using a good range of well-chosen vocabulary.

Total: 14/15 marks

Answering Question 2

In Question 2, you are asked to read Text C and discuss the writer's craft in different ways.

Start by carefully Re-reading the information about Text C (it is in italics above the text) to make sure you understand it. This will tell you what genre the text is (fiction or non-fiction) and may give you information on the setting and location.

Then go back to the questions. Annotate the extracts from the text according to each sub-question. You will find some alternative words or ways of explaining what the author has written, but you must keep to the text.

As there may be no single correct answer, you must always support your views with examples from the text to prove each point you make.

 Apply

1 Study how another student prepared to answer Question 2 below.

2 Go back to page 18 and answer Question 2(c) and (d) yourself.

3 Compare your answers with the student's answers and examiner comments on pages 29–30.

Preparing to answer Question 2

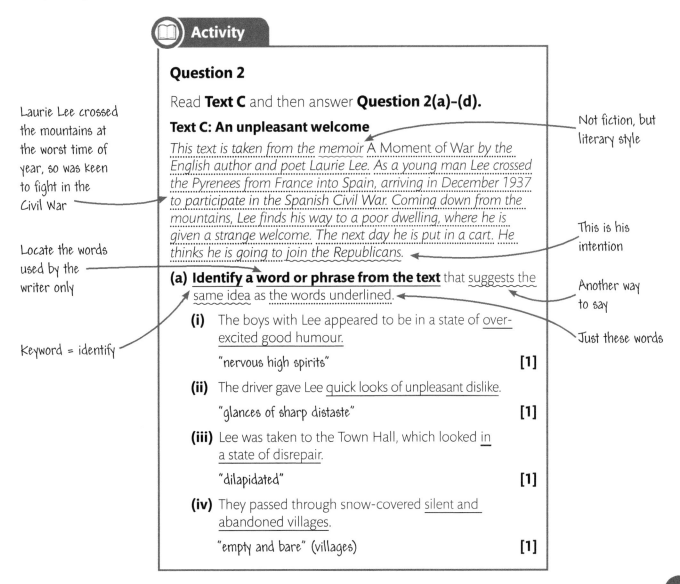

Activity

Question 2

Read **Text C** and then answer **Question 2(a)–(d)**.

Text C: An unpleasant welcome

This text is taken from the memoir A Moment of War by the English author and poet Laurie Lee. As a young man Lee crossed the Pyrenees from France into Spain, arriving in December 1937 to participate in the Spanish Civil War. Coming down from the mountains, Lee finds his way to a poor dwelling, where he is given a strange welcome. The next day he is put in a cart. He thinks he is going to join the Republicans.

(a) **Identify a word or phrase from the text** that suggests the same idea as the words underlined.

(i) The boys with Lee appeared to be in a state of over-excited good humour.

"nervous high spirits" **[1]**

(ii) The driver gave Lee quick looks of unpleasant dislike.

"glances of sharp distaste" **[1]**

(iii) Lee was taken to the Town Hall, which looked in a state of disrepair.

"dilapidated" **[1]**

(iv) They passed through snow-covered silent and abandoned villages.

"empty and bare" (villages) **[1]**

Annotations (handwritten):
- Laurie Lee crossed the mountains at the worst time of year, so was keen to fight in the Civil War
- Not fiction, but literary style
- This is his intention
- Locate the words used by the writer only
- Another way to say
- Just these words
- Keyword = identify

Joking/making fun?

Like birds/edge of seats and holding guns – nervous?

Simile

Keyword = explain the writer's intentions

Discuss literary techniques – writer's craft and implicit meanings

Exam tip

Show off your knowledge and use of English by demonstrating how well you can identify and use literary language in your answers to Question 2(c) and (d).

Something terrible has happened here/sense of foreboding

A form of foreshadowing – the frightening/ unpleasant experience that is about to come

Read the correct paragraph!

Keyword = explain

Find 3 words/phrases that give the overall impression or create an atmosphere

---

(b) Using your own words, explain what the writer means by each of the words underlined.

I was beginning to get a bit bored with all this levity, and sat there silent and shivering. The boys perched close beside me, one on each side, holding their guns at the ready, like sentries. Every so often they pointed them at me and nodded brightly. They appeared to be in a state of nervous high spirits.

(i) levity

joking and teasing [1]

(ii) perched

sat on the edge of the seat [1]

(iii) sentries

like soldiers on duty [1]

(c) Use **one** example of a word or phrase from the text below to explain how the writer suggests he is going to have a much harder time in Spain than he had expected. **Use your own words in your explanation.**

Through the iced winter morning, slipping over glassy rocks, we made our stumbling way down the valley, passing snow-covered villages, empty and bare, from which all life and sound seemed withdrawn. This chilling silence was surely not one of nature, which could be broken by a goat-bell or the chirp of a bird. It was as if a paralysing pestilence had visited the place, and I was to notice it on a number of occasions in the weeks to come.

[3]

(d) Re-read paragraphs 7 and 8.

- Paragraph 7 begins "Through the iced winter morning ..." and tells of Lee's journey on the cart.

- Paragraph 8 begins "After an hour or so ..." and is about arriving in a small hill town.

Explain how the writer uses language to convey meaning and to create effect in these paragraphs.

Choose **three** examples of words or phrases from **each** paragraph to support your answer. Your choices should include the use of imagery.

Write about 200–300 words.

Rephrase to show my use of English

Keyword = explain

In this context/for this story

Simile – they are not actually 'sentries'

How does the writer gives this impression?

Suggests something unnatural and that this was a more populated place before (why have people left?)

Unnatural – chill/cold fear

Lee gets an impression or feeling

Alliteration for powerful phrase

Identify words in the paragraphs, draw them together and examine the combined effect

What effects do the writer's words have on me?

Quote the examples to justify ideas/feelings

Important!

Sample answer 2(c)–(d) and examiner comments

Now study the student's answers to Question 2(c) and (d) and examiner comments on the answers. You will see that the student has crossed through some sections to keep to the correct word count and the examiner has highlighted appropriate points.

> **Exam tip**
>
> - Write in clear sentences and remember to punctuate quotations.
> - Examiners can give you more marks if you comment on the effects created by a writer's use of grammar, syntax and punctuation, but this must be in addition to your comments on the writer's use of words.

 Activity

Question 2(c)

The phrase "chilling silence" combines two aspects of why Lee is going to have a harder time in Spain than he anticipated. The weather is very cold and he is not dressed or prepared for it. The silence is because people have moved out of the villages and area and there are no living creatures, either. No cows or farm animals, which seems strange. I think Lee was expecting a 'warm welcome' and he gets the opposite. Nobody wants him and the weather is bad.

 Examiner comments

2/3 marks

An appropriate example and attempt at an explanation that shows some understanding of how the writer suggests his situation and experience, but does not discuss his choice of words (adjective + noun) adequately for full marks.

 Activity

Question 2(d)

Laurie Lee creates a silent, desolate mountain landscape in paragraph 7. There is a "chilling silence"; no birds or animals can be heard. The author uses the word "numbness" and we get a sense that there is a sort of "numbness" in the people and the land itself, like when your hands are so cold you can't feel them anymore. Lee gives a strong ~~image~~ impression of how barren and lifeless the place is through his use of imagery. Especially in a powerful alliteration, ~~in a~~ "paralysing pestilence". The combination of visual and aural imagery creates a sense of foreboding. This leads up to an unexpected and frightening situation in paragraph 8. Lee is nervous about the fact that the two boys on the cart with him are carrying guns and treat him like a prisoner, but in this paragraph they "grow nervous and tense", suggesting anything could happen or that they may be taking him to be shot. Lee is building a sense of tension and when the cart enters the town two militiamen "marched ahead" of it, as if taking Lee to the scaffold. Lee has been expecting a warm welcome and what he gets is a terrifyingly cold reception in both the land and the people. This all leads up to four soldiers coming for him with "fixed bayonets". The reader is made tense and nervous in paragraph 7, and this leads up to sharing Lee's frightening situation in paragraph 8. We now want to read on to find out what happens to Laurie Lee. He conveys his memory of his feelings when he was young by making us share his emotions ~~and~~ so we empathise with him. It is more like reading exciting fiction than a memoir or autobiography. (288 words)

Shows understanding of meaning and use of language

Good choice of example and understands writer's intentions

Perceptive and analytical

Shows how writer builds tension

Interprets very well

Shows understanding of empathy and understands writer's intentions

Good

Shows understanding of the genre

Examiner comments

14/15 marks

Student selects powerful and unusual words ("numbness") and demonstrates very good understanding of how and why the language is effective in the context of the extract. Sound understanding of implicit and explicit meanings. Good explanation of literary features, use of imagery and explanations of how the writer uses this for visual and aural effect. Comment on "building tension" shows excellent understanding of the writer's intentions and craft. Aware of genre and use of language in fiction.

Exam tip

Use your knowledge of the writer's craft to help you create the setting and location in your answer.

Answering Question 3

This question asks you to respond to **Text C** in a particular way and write in a particular style. You could be asked to write a letter, a report, a journal, a speech, an interview or an article.

You will be assessed on your reading and your writing skills. You need to demonstrate that you can understand explicit and implicit meaning and attitudes, and that you can analyse and develop Text C in your own writing.

 Apply

1 Look below at how another student has keyworded the question and identified details in the text.
2 Then go back to page 19 and answer Question 3 yourself.
3 Compare your answer with the student's answers and examiner comments on pages 32–3. The marking guidelines for this question are at the back of the book on page 202.

Exam tip

- You must address each bullet point in the question so find a way to incorporate them into your answer. In an interview you could rephrase them as the interviewer's questions. In a letter, journal entry or speech you could re-word them as topic sentences. In a report or an article, they can be reworded as subheadings. Make sure you plan and sequence your answer around the bullet points.
- Creating a personality for the persona (fictitious person) will help you to develop thoughts and feelings that suit Text C. Re-read the text from the point of view of the person you are being asked to be. This will help you to describe events and feelings in a more effective way. Use the text and develop your writing according to how you felt then and how you feel now.
- Show off your knowledge and use of English by demonstrating how well you can identify and use literary language in your answer.

Preparing to answer Question 3

Look at how a student has keyworded Question 3 and annotated Text C for the extended response question.

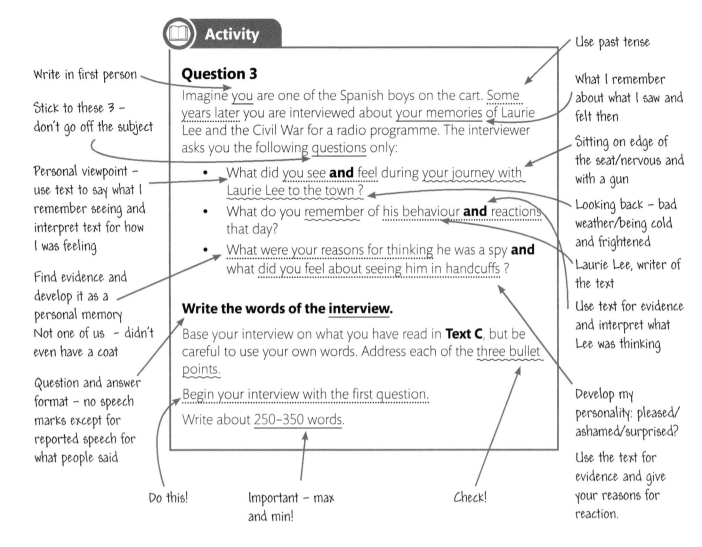

Write in first person

Stick to these 3 – don't go off the subject

Personal viewpoint – use text to say what I remember seeing and interpret text for how I was feeling

Find evidence and develop it as a personal memory
Not one of us – didn't even have a coat

Question and answer format – no speech marks except for reported speech for what people said

Activity

Question 3

Imagine you are one of the Spanish boys on the cart. Some years later you are interviewed about your memories of Laurie Lee and the Civil War for a radio programme. The interviewer asks you the following questions only:

- What did you see **and** feel during your journey with Laurie Lee to the town ?
- What do you remember of his behaviour **and** reactions that day?
- What were your reasons for thinking he was a spy **and** what did you feel about seeing him in handcuffs ?

Write the words of the interview.

Base your interview on what you have read in **Text C**, but be careful to use your own words. Address each of the three bullet points.

Begin your interview with the first question.

Write about 250–350 words.

Use past tense

What I remember about what I saw and felt then

Sitting on edge of the seat/nervous and with a gun

Looking back – bad weather/being cold and frightened

Laurie Lee, writer of the text

Use text for evidence and interpret what Lee was thinking

Develop my personality: pleased/ashamed/surprised?

Use the text for evidence and give your reasons for reaction.

Do this!   Important – max and min!   Check!

Text C: An unpleasant welcome

Surprised to see Lee

In winter!

Violin could be the spy's cover story

Cart for carrying prisoners to executions

There was a motionless silence while they took me in – seeing a young tattered stranger, coatless and soaked to the knees, carrying a kit-bag from which a violin bow protruded. Suddenly the old woman said "Ay!" and beckoned me to the fire, which was piled high with glowing pine cones. I crouched, thawing out by the choking fumes, sensing deeply this moment of arrival. [...]

[The next morning] the boys half-marched me into the lane and the rest of the family followed and stood watching, blowing on their purple fingers. [...] The cart waiting in the lane resembled a rough-looking tumbril, and the driver had a cavernous, nervous face. "Vamanos, vamanos, vamanos," he kept muttering plaintively, giving me glances of sharp distaste. The boys helped me into the back of the cart and climbed up after me.

"Here he is. The English one," they said with ponderous jocularity. The driver sniffed, and uncoiled his whip.

"Horse and cart," said one of the brothers, nudging me smartly. "We've got to save your legs. They must be half destroyed with all this

She felt sorry for him

Really cold

Why did I help him?

Trying to make a joke of it – but did I have doubts?

Why this sarcasm? Whose side is Lee on?

Did it feel as if I was taking a prisoner to jail?

Lee is a nuisance and the old man doesn't want to drive him

Why?

Took a long time to get to town in icy, mountainous conditions

What I saw

Wordless before, now sits up as if doing something important

Does Lee smile here? Interpret his feelings

What I said

How did this feel – any regrets?

Perched because very uncomfortable but also because I was nervous?

I was pleased about catching a spy

Did Lee really walk or was he dropped off by transport?

Do I remember unnatural silence (too nervy)?

What I saw

Men in uniform (a real war)

Was I expecting this?

Was I proud of what we'd done? How did I feel later?

---

walking over mountains. And what have we got if we haven't got your legs? You wouldn't be much use to us, would you?"

I was beginning to get a bit bored with all this levity, and sat there silent and shivering. The boys perched close beside me, one on each side, holding their guns at the ready, like sentries. Every so often they pointed them at me and nodded brightly. They appeared to be in a state of nervous high spirits.

"Vamanos!" snarled the driver and shook up the reins crossly. The old man and his wife raised their hands solemnly and told me to go with God. The little girl threw a stone at the horse, or it may have been at me, but it hit the horse and caused it to start with a jerk. So we began to lumber and creak down the steep rocky lane, the brothers now holding me by either elbow. The Pyrenees stood high behind us, white and hard, their peaks colouring to the rising sun. The boys nodded towards them, grinning, nudging me sharply again, and baring their chestnut-tinted teeth.

Through the iced winter morning, slipping over glassy rocks, we made our stumbling way down the valley, passing snow-covered villages, empty and bare, from which all life and sound seemed withdrawn. This chilling silence was surely not one of nature, which could be broken by a goat-bell or the chirp of a bird. It was as if a paralysing pestilence had visited the place, and I was to notice it on a number of occasions in the weeks to come. It was simply the stupefying numbness of war.

After an hour or so we came to a small hill town still shuttered by the shadow of rocks. A bent woman crept by, bearing a great load of firewood. A cat shot through a hole in a wall. I noticed that the brothers had suddenly grown tense and anxious, sitting straight as pillars, thin-lipped, beside me. Two militiamen, in khaki ponchos, came out of a doorway and marched ahead of us down the street. Even our driver perked up and began to look around him with what appeared to be an air of importance. The militiamen led us into the square, to the dilapidated Town Hall, from which the Republican flag was hanging. The brothers called out to a couple of sentries who were sitting on the steps, and one of them got up and went inside. Now for a proper welcome, I thought. I got down from the cart, and the brothers followed. Then four soldiers came out with fixed bayonets.

"We've brought you the spy," said the brothers, and pushed me forward. The soldiers closed round me and handcuffed my wrists.

Sample answer 3 and examiner comments

 Activity

Question 3

Interviewer (Int): Tell us what you saw and felt during your journey with Laurie Lee to the town that day?

Me: It was a very long time ago but I remember how cold it was. Lee was shaking, but it might have been the cold, he only had a jacket, no

Shows thoughts

Shows feelings

Develops thoughts

Rephrases bullet points well

Implied content – good

Is this deliberate – farm boy's bad grammar?

Imagines – good

Develops idea

Interprets

In retrospect – good

Good interpretation

winter coat or hat or even any gloves. I don't think he was frightened, though. Not until later. It was a really hard winter, everything was icey. We didn't see anyone until we got to the town, either. Only a bent old woman gathering firewood, poor old thing. Can't have been easy with all her menfolk away fighting. Villages were deserted.

Int: Can you remember anything about his behaviour and reactions that day?

Me: Well, like I said, he didn't seem frightened until we got to the town. I don't think he knew we thought he was a spy. We kept on nudgeing him to get a reaction and all he did was sit silent, although I think he understood what we were saying. Must of done if he'd come to Spain to fight. He just sat looking about him until we got to the town, then we all got more nervous. He gulped hard when he saw the men with the bayonets but I don't think he realised he was going to be their prisoner.

Int: Why did you think he was a spy? What did you feel about seeing him in handcuffs?

Me: ~~We thought he was spy because~~ He'd come over from France and he was a foreignor and he had a violin! As if he was going to pretend to play it in the street or cafés and watch what was going on. He looked educated too not like a farm boy like me. Not having a coat or hat was suspicious. Like he'd been brought by a car not come over the mountains on foot. I felt sorry for him though. When they put him in handcuffs he looked really surprised but not in a nice way. I just wanted to get back to our house those militiamen were scarey. (350 words)

✓ Examiner comments

Reading: 13/15 marks

A thorough evaluation and analysis of the text. Ideas are developed, supported and sustained. Each point relates well to the text. Supporting detail is evident and integrated into the writing. There is a sense of purpose and the approach is appropriate. All three bullets (copied in) are well covered. A convincing voice is used.

Writing: 8/10 marks

The register is effective for the purpose. The language sounds convincing and appropriate. Ideas are expressed in a wide range of vocabulary. The structure is a little weak for top marks, but otherwise it is well-sequenced (using bullet points copied from question). Poor grammar is possibly deliberate for the point of view ("must of ..."). Otherwise it is easy to follow and well-focused.

Total: 21/25 marks

Review

Think about how you approached the Paper 1 questions and tasks in this unit. Use the questionnaire over the page to review your progress and what you need to do to progress further.

The part I find most challenging in Paper 1 is Question ...	
Annotating a text helps because ...	
Were the sample answers similar to mine? If not, why not?	
I need to practise ...	
I need to revise ...	
I need to get help to improve ...	

Raise your grade

Fill out the questionnaire below to assess your progress, then make notes on what you can do to raise your grade.

	Struggling	Improve	Good
Reading skills			
I can identify words and phrases with specific meanings.			
I can write alternative words and phrases to those given in Question 1.			
I understand the difference between facts and opinions.			
I can identify how and why ideas and opinions are being used.			
I can select and use details for a specific purpose in a summary.			
Discussing the writer's craft in Question 2			
I can identify different writing styles.			
I can explain why a writer has used certain words.			
I can explain register and tone.			
I can identify what a writer (or fictional character) thinks, feels and imagines.			
I can explain how a text has been written, why specific words have been chosen and what effect this has on readers.			
I can identifiy why different sentence structures have been used for certain effects.			
Writing the extended response for Question 3			
I can see how another person might think or feel (for Question 3).			
I can use a wide range of vocabulary for an extended writing task.			

What I can do to raise my grade	
I can raise my marks in Question 1 by …	
I can raise my marks in Question 2 by …	
I can raise my marks in Question 3 by …	
I am fairly confident about …	
I am less confident about …	
My target grade for Paper 1 is …	

Objectives

In this unit you will:

- Explore what is in Paper 2
- Explore what examiners are looking for
- Plan and write different types of Directed Writing
- Plan and write your own narrative and descriptive compositions
- Review your progress and how to raise your grade

During your course, you will have developed your writing skills by reading a range of texts and responding to them in various styles for different purposes and audiences in Directed Writing tasks. This has included writing letters, reports, journal entries, articles and speeches. You have developed your creative writing skills to entertain and inform in narrative and descriptive compositions. Now you are being asked to show how well you understand the writer's craft and how well you can use language to achieve certain effects.

This unit will help you to understand the different types of question in Paper 2, the assessment objectives and what examiners are looking for in your answers. Work through the unit, then answer the review questions at the end to monitor your progress.

Preparing for Paper 2 involves improving your writing skills so that you are more effective at:

- keywording questions for composition tasks
- annotating texts for Directed Writing tasks
- writing to inform, argue and persuade
- writing to inform and entertain in narrative and descriptive compositions.

What is in Paper 2

Paper 2 is divided into Sections A and B.

- Section A (Directed Writing) contains Question 1, which is compulsory, and refers to one or two texts, which are printed in a separate insert.
- Section B (Composition) contains Questions 2–5 and you must choose **one** to answer.

Section A: Directed Writing

You will be asked to read either one or two texts totalling 650–750 words in length. Question 1, which is compulsory, asks you to evaluate the content of the text(s) to create a discursive, argumentative or persuasive speech, letter or article. Your answer will be about 250–350 words.

Question 1 is worth a total of 40 marks: 15 marks for the content of your answer (demonstrating your reading skills) and 25 marks for the quality of your writing.

 Review

Paper 2 Directed Writing and Composition is optional

All students take *either* Paper 2 *or* Component 3. This part of the Cambridge IGCSE First Language English exam is to show how well you can read, understand and respond to different types of text in a compulsory Directed Writing task. You will also be asked to write a narrative or a descriptive composition.

Exam tip

Organising your time for Paper 2

Aim to spend one hour on each section, but leave yourself time to review both answers before the end of the exam.

 QuestionRecap

Directed Writing to discuss sets out a balanced, objective analysis of a subject or situation. It can be used in reports and informative articles, and can also form the basis of an interview or journal entry.

QuestionRecap

Directed Writing to argue presents two sides of an argument and argues why one, in your opinion, is better than the other. It can be used in letters, speeches or articles.

Directed Writing to persuade sets out two or more sides to a subject or situation and persuades the audience to one way of thinking. It can be used in letters and speeches.

 Link

You can find more information on writing to discuss, argue and persuade in Unit 3 of this book.

 **QuestionRecap**

Descriptive compositions

- are not in story form – they go straight to the subject, situation, event or location
- are written from a first-person perspective
- include imagery for particular effects
- can be a factual account but must not become a story.

Narrative compositions

- are in story form with a beginning, a middle and an end
- can be told from the first-person or third-person perspective
- can be entirely fictitious or an account based on fact – details of a real event can be exaggerated or retold in a way to have a particular effect on the reader
- include characters and often dialogue, direct thought and indirect thought.

Assessment objectives

Question 1 also tests your reading skills. You need to show how well you:

- understand explicit meanings in the text(s)
- understand implicit meanings and attitudes
- analyse, evaluate and develop facts, ideas and opinions
- support your views or argument by selecting and using relevant information from the text(s).

Question 1 tests your writing skills. You need to show how well you:

- articulate experiences and express what you think, feel and imagine
- organise and structure your ideas and opinions for a deliberate effect or purpose
- use your vocabulary and different sentence structures
- use a register appropriate to the context of your composition
- spell and use punctuation and grammar correctly.

Section B: Composition

There are four questions in Section B: two for descriptive compositions and two for narrative compositions. You only need to answer one question and will need to write about 350–450 words.

This question is worth a total of 40 marks: 16 marks for the content and structure of your answer and 24 marks for the style and accuracy of your writing.

Assessment objectives

These questions test your writing skills. You need to show how well you:

- articulate and express what you think, feel and imagine
- order and present facts, ideas and opinions for a deliberate effect
- make accurate and effective use of paragraphs
- use a range of appropriate vocabulary
- use a variety of sentence structures
- use language and register appropriate to your audience and context
- use accurate spelling and correct punctuation and grammar.

Sample Paper 2, Section A

Read the sample paper extract below before moving on to the next sections.

 Text A: Seasteads for survival

This is a blog post about finding solutions for coastal communities around the world that are under threat from rising sea levels.

There used to be an entire floating town in Hong Kong's Causeway Bay. Tens of thousands of boat-dwellers lived there, forming a self-sufficient district entirely on water. They were members of the Tanka

QuestionRecap

Take about 10–15 minutes to read the text, before you turn to the question.

5   community, whose ancestors had become fishermen after abandoning a life of warfare on land. They were also considered social outcasts and forbidden to even step ashore until the middle of the last century, but if you think about it, as rising sea levels threaten

10   existing coastal cities, living on a boat has major advantages – whether you are a social outcast or not.

It may sound like science fiction but, as rising sea levels become an ever more serious threat to low-lying cities and island nations around the world,

15   neighbourhoods like this could become common. At present, most coastal cities are strengthening and extending their sea defences, but there are others that are beginning to explore alternative solutions to help them survive approaching tides and even benefit

20   from them.

A floating village at London's Royal Docks has got the official go-ahead and Rotterdam has a Rijnhaven waterfront development well under way. Eventually, whole neighbourhoods of water-threatened land

25   could be floating out to sea. It has taken years of discussions and small-scale experiments, but the floating solution is finally being seen as the sensible thing to do.

But how will these towns feed themselves? Well,

30   you've heard of fish farms and farmsteads, what about *seasteads*? A seastead could be a village community farming the sea to feed itself. Create a floating village on a cruise ship (they're big enough) or transform an oil-platform and you have got

35   space for living accommodation. Maintenance jobs will have to be done to keep the ship or platform functioning, and people will need to work on domestic issues such as cleaning and refuse collection, but other people could become fish farmers.

40   New seasteaders who can't cope with this lifestyle or have problems with their neighbours can simply return to land or find another floating home. Ideally, and if sea levels keep on rising, there will be all sorts of seasteads floating off the coasts of different

45   countries. They probably won't be Utopias, but they will offer a place for people to live away from over-crowded inland city areas. It's all about making our planet better, cleaner and healthier. Above all, seasteads could help to ensure humanity has a future.

50   Current estimates for the potential rise in sea levels

Exam tip

You can annotate the text and use any space for planning, but do not write your answer on the insert.

Exam tip

Write your answers in the spaces provided. If you need more space, use extra sheets of paper, numbering your answers clearly.

55 due to climate change vary widely, but many islands are under threat. The Maldives, for example, consist of atoll islands a mere two metres above sea level: islands such as these could be inundated and completely uninhabitable within our lifetime. This could end their national existence entirely, but if they recreate their communities on ocean-going vessels or platforms there's a way to escape destruction.

60 Naturally, there are financial matters to consider. Initially, seasteading is going to be very expensive. Building platforms to house hundreds of people will take time and special building materials. Regular, essential maintenance costs will also be high. Then there are the problems of providing heat and energy:

65 electricity is expected to be approximately two and a half times as expensive as on land.

While seasteading offers a way for island states to escape the consequences of rising sea levels, it may prove too expensive and complicated for large

70 communities as a whole. But the chances of smaller groups on floating fish-farm villages surviving and being successful are fairly good. These would be aquaculture communities that literally harvest the sea.

The actual building and maintenance of a seastead –

75 or converting a ship or oil rig – will be a major social and engineering challenge. Once comfortable and secure accommodation has been created there are still all the arrangements for supplies, ferries, Internet, medical care and so on to be made. However, as

80 a way of surviving the future, it is something our generation needs to explore. We need to make plans for where we are going to be in fifty years' time, above or below sea-level.

 **Activity**

Read **Text A, _Seasteads for survival_**, and then answer **Section A, Question 1.**

Question 1

Imagine you live in a small community very close to the coast. Your village is being threatened by rising sea levels. You read this blog article (Text A) about rising sea levels and seasteads, and decide seasteading is something your community should consider.

Write a speech to persuade the members of your community to consider the idea of seasteading. Give your views on why moving onto a floating platform or into a converted cruise ship is a good idea and how you all might benefit.

In your speech you should:

• give your views on whether a floating village is possible

- explain how it could benefit your community
- evaluate the challenges of living out at sea.

Base your speech on what you have read in **Text A**, but be careful to use your own words. Address all the bullet points.

Begin your speech: "Thank you for coming to listen to me today …"

Write about 250–350 words.

Up to 15 marks are available for the content of your answer, and up to 25 marks for the quality of your writing.

Preparing to answer Section A, Question 1

 Apply

1 Re-read the sample paper extract above. Read Text A first, then Question 1.

2 Start your preparation by keywording the question to find out exactly what you are being asked to do.

3 Then annotate the text in response to the question. There are about 20 different points you can use and develop in your answer. Count the points you found in the text and number them in the order you would use them.

4 Make notes on how you might begin and end your speech for best effect.

 Link

You can find more on keywording questions on page 21 of this book and on page 6 of the *Complete First Language English for Cambridge IGCSE® Student Book.*

Your keywording of Question 1 should have identified the following:

- What you are being asked to do and who is the audience. You must *persuade* your community to consider the possibility of living on a seastead, including how this could benefit them and evaluating the challenges involved.
- How you are being asked to write – the format and the style. You must write in an appropriate style for a speech.
- You must begin your speech with the words: "Thank you for coming to listen to me today …" and base it on what you have read in Text A, using your own words.
- You must address all the bullet points. What details must you include?
- You must write a minimum of 250 words and a maximum of 350 words.

 Link

You can revise the features of speech writing in Unit 6 of the *Complete First Language English for Cambridge IGCSE® Student Book.*

Aristotle's three "strands of persuasion" are on page 145 of the *Complete First Language English for Cambridge IGCSE® Student Book.*

What examiners are looking for

 Apply

1 Read two students' answers on pages 42–3. Then make notes on how well each student has met the basic assessment criteria on page 42

2 Look at the assessment guidelines for Directed Writing (Table A and Table B) on page 203 to see what examiners are looking for and how they award marks.

3 Then turn to pages 43–4 and look at how an examiner marked Student A's speech.

Basic assessment criteria
Content
- Have all the bullet points been addressed? (If not, what is missing?)
- Is there evidence of planning?
- Have paragraphs been structured to lead up to a sound conclusion? (Look for topic sentences.)

Style and quality of writing
- Is the composition written in the appropriate style for a persuasive speech?
- Does the student use their own words? Is there a good range of vocabulary?
- Does the student vary sentence structures?
- Is the writing grammatically correct?
- Has the composition been corrected (proofread)? (Check the spelling and punctuation.)

Sample answers Section A, Question 1

 Activity

Question 1, Student A

Thank you for coming to listen to me today because we have a problem but I have a solution that will save our community, save our children, and save our skins, instead of moving inland and getting crowded or worse washed away we actually move out to see. We can buy a cruise ship and set it up as our floating village. A cruise ship is the perfect answer because they have cafeterias, medical facillities, even discos and even a library for people to read books in.

Instead of spending money on road repairs and other community expenses what we should do is spend it on buying an old cruise ship. The people who work for the council can then work on the ship. When it's all ready – we'll have combine cabins into appartments – then we can move in and sail away before the sea level reaches our village. People who run cafes and restaurants now can run there businesses on the ship. Doctors and nurses can be doctors and nurses in the medical facilities on the ship. Cooks and cleaners can keep the same jobs. Even lawyers and teachers. We'll need a school so we can convert a space in the ship into classrooms. Children can play on deck like tourists do on the cruise ships. It'll be great.

Taking animals might be a problem it isn't going to be a noah's ark but they'll be alright living wild so you can set them free when we go. We'll have to have plenty of food because we can't live on fish all the time so we should start stockpilling it now. Rice and flour and dry goods and electricians can make sure the freezers and fridges keep working so we can take plenty of meat and eggs. We can keep hens of course and rabbits and some goats for milk even cows if you like.

So what do you think? Is this a good idea or what! (328 words)

 Activity

Question 1, Student B

Thank you for coming to listen to me today. We are facing the most dangerous time of our lives against an enemy we can't defeat – the sea. ~~But there's a sollution and allthough some of you are going to laugh I believe you should take it seriously.~~

The sea level is rising all around our island. We are losing land that our ancestor's ~~cultivated and~~ made prosper. Soon we will have no alternative but to move to towns inland unless we ~~take drastic action~~ find an alternative. We are people of the sea, not city-dwellers – so I want you to consider moving onto a floating platform or a converted cruise ship and living at sea. In the past we've had land to farm and produce to eat: now we should consider farming the sea instead.

Feeding our community is going to be top priority, but if we store goods and learn more about how to exploit the sea we will be fine. Those of us who don't like it can move back onto dry land if they want to. If we convert a ship or an oil rig we'll be creating jobs as well for engineers, electricians and builders and painters etc. How we pay each other is something to be sorted out but basically everything we do will be for our community. It will be helping us to save ourselves in a catastrophe and more importantly save the existence of our community as a group for our children.

It is going to be a challenge but it's a wonderful opportunity so we should face it with a positive approach. We can ~~even~~ sell fish to people on shore and make a profit then use this money for supplies and improvements.

You see it is possible! It is the sensible thing to do! Our floating village will provide security, it'll provide a means of feeding ourselves, it will provide a way of ensuring we stay together for our children's benefit.

Yes, we have to face challenges and expense, yes, we have to find the money to pay for it and at times we might fall out, but decide where you want to be in 50 year's time and let's get started NOW! (346 words)

Examiner comments

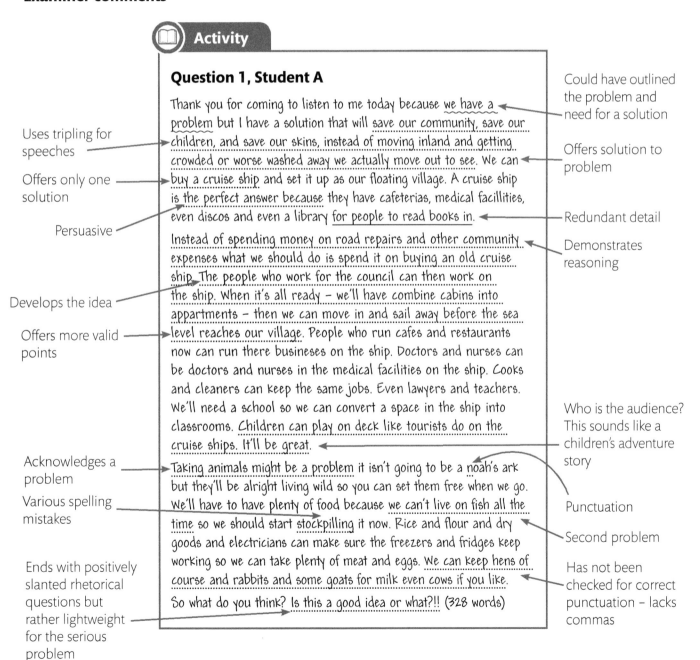

Activity

Question 1, Student A

Thank you for coming to listen to me today because we have a problem but I have a solution that will save our community, save our children, and save our skins, instead of moving inland and getting crowded or worse washed away we actually move out to see. We can buy a cruise ship and set it up as our floating village. A cruise ship is the perfect answer because they have cafeterias, medical facillities, even discos and even a library for people to read books in.

Instead of spending money on road repairs and other community expenses what we should do is spend it on buying an old cruise ship. The people who work for the council can then work on the ship. When it's all ready – we'll have combine cabins into appartments – then we can move in and sail away before the sea level reaches our village. People who run cafes and restaurants now can run there businesses on the ship. Doctors and nurses can be doctors and nurses in the medical facilities on the ship. Cooks and cleaners can keep the same jobs. Even lawyers and teachers. We'll need a school so we can convert a space in the ship into classrooms. Children can play on deck like tourists do on the cruise ships. It'll be great.

Taking animals might be a problem it isn't going to be a noah's ark but they'll be alright living wild so you can set them free when we go. We'll have to have plenty of food because we can't live on fish all the time so we should start stockpilling it now. Rice and flour and dry goods and electricians can make sure the freezers and fridges keep working so we can take plenty of meat and eggs. We can keep hens of course and rabbits and some goats for milk even cows if you like.

So what do you think? Is this a good idea or what?!! (328 words)

Left-hand comments:

Uses tripling for speeches

Offers only one solution

Persuasive

Develops the idea

Offers more valid points

Acknowledges a problem

Various spelling mistakes

Ends with positively slanted rhetorical questions but rather lightweight for the serious problem

Right-hand comments:

Could have outlined the problem and need for a solution

Offers solution to problem

Redundant detail

Demonstrates reasoning

Who is the audience? This sounds like a children's adventure story

Punctuation

Second problem

Has not been checked for correct punctuation – lacks commas

Examiner comments

Question 1, Student A

Overall effect: Student has answered the question in the appropriate style but overlooked important aspects of the bullet points. There is no attempt to clarify the problem facing the community and no significant evaluation of how the challenges of moving onto a ship will benefit the community other than "saving (their) skins". There is very little evidence of planning the writing.

Reading: 5/15 marks

Shows basic understanding of explicit meanings but only limited understanding of implicit meanings and attitudes. Fails to analyse, evaluate and develop facts, ideas and opinions, using appropriate support from the text effectively (does not develop the text to discuss the problems of an entire community living on a ship apart from those related to food and animals). Selects and uses information for a specific purpose at a superficial level (an "adventure").

Writing: 14/25 marks

Articulates and expresses what is thought, felt and imagined (very enthusiastic), but fails to support own argument with sound ideas, although opinions are given for a deliberate effect. Uses a relatively wide range of vocabulary and sentence structures generally appropriate to the context, but there are too many run-on phrases, showing lack of proofreading and editing. The style and register are appropriate to the context. There are numerous spelling and punctuation mistakes.

Total: 19/40 marks

✏ Apply

1 Look at the marking guidelines for Directed Writing (Table A and Table B) on page 203. Mark Student B's speech yourself. You can annotate the speech on pages 42–3 and write your "examiner comments" below.

....

....

....

....

....

....

....

....

....

....

2 Look at page 45 to see what marks an examiner gave it.

Examiner comments

Question 1, Student B

Overall effect: Student B has answered the question in the appropriate style, using the bullet points as guidelines. There is some evaluation of how moving onto a ship will benefit the community and of the challenges involved. Develops an argument in a logical and persuasive manner. Has cut the wording to keep to the word limit and maintained the flow of the argument well. Paragraphs lead to a satisfactory conclusion.

Reading: 12/15 marks

Shows good understanding of explicit meanings and sound understanding of implicit meanings and attitudes. Analyses, evaluates and develops facts, ideas and opinions, using appropriate but only basic support from the text. Selects and uses information for a specific (persuasive) purpose.

Writing: 18/25 marks

Somewhat repetitive and uses limited vocabulary but articulates and expresses what is thought, felt and imagined. Supports the argument with sound ideas and uses opinions for a deliberate effect. The style uses emotive and persuasive language (past/present/future technique). Sentence structures are basically sound and appropriate to the context, as is the register. There are a few overlooked spelling and punctuation mistakes, so the speech was not checked adequately, possibly because of cutting words and running out of time.

Total: 30/40 marks

Planning your Directed Writing

Planning your writing is very important. For the Directed Writing task, the style may differ depending on whether you are asked to write a discursive, argumentative or persuasive letter, article or speech. The content must relate to what is in the Section A text(s) and how you develop it. Your planning will make sure that you address the bullet points, develop information from the text and write effectively in an appropriate style. Good planning also helps to raise your grade.

Keywording the question and annotating the text

You are already familiar with the first stage of planning your Directed Writing: keyword the question and annotate the text to select information you want to use. Do the activity below to refine these skills for Directed Writing.

 QuestionRecap

When you annotate the text to select information, use a pencil or coloured pencils to help you start to organise your ideas.

Apply

1 Look at another Directed Writing task over the page. Read the text at least twice to understand its content, then read and keyword the question on page 47.

2 Decide on your opinion. Are you for or against circuses?

3 Look at the bullet points in the question and decide how you can use them in your article. Annotate the question with your ideas.

4 Re-read and annotate the text, selecting information to support your argument.

5 Then turn to pages 48–9 to see how this text can be used to identify details for two different points of view.

Link

You can revise the features of articles in Unit 7 of the *Complete First Language English for Cambridge IGCSE® Student Book* and you can recap Writing to argue and persuade on page 39.

Text B: A short history of the travelling circus

https://circus-historians.com

This is an Internet article from a website about circuses.

The circus as an entertainment goes back to very ancient origins. In Ancient Rome, the "circus" was a location for watching horse and chariot races, staged battles and displays of trained animals. The travelling circus as we know it, however, started in England during the 1770s, when Philip Astley, an ex-cavalry war veteran, brought acrobatics,
5   riding and clowning together in a ring at his riding school near Westminster Bridge in London. The equestrian performances included trick-riding, bareback acrobatics, dressage and "liberty acts", with horses running loose in the ring.

During the 19th century, equestrians, male and female, were the true stars of the circus, although floor acrobats were beginning to make their mark. The best acrobats were often
10   clowns. At this time, circus clowns were essentially mimics who could also sing, ride a horse, juggle, present trained animals, do balancing acts or tumble. An English clown called Little Wheal became famous for regularly performing a hundred consecutive somersaults, which was quite a feat then or now.

Tightrope walkers, who were the undisputed stars of travelling fairs, were among the
15   first professional acrobats to appear in the circus ring. They adapted their acts to become one of any circus's most prized attractions: the trapeze. This began with swinging from a slack rope, then a bar was added with vertical ropes on each side. In 1859, the French gymnast, Jules Léotard presented an act at the Cirque Napoléon in Paris in which he jumped from one trapeze to another. Léotard had invented the flying trapeze, for which
20   he became the toast of Europe, and was the originator of a costume still used today by acrobats and dancers – the leotard.

By the close of the 19th century, railways and automobiles were replacing horses on the roads and equestrian displays were losing their supremacy to exotic animals, especially big cats. Some trained exotic animals had appeared earlier in circus history, around 1812.
25   At the Cirque Olympique in Paris, the Franconis presented Kioumi, the first trained elephant, but it was a later combination of circus and menagerie that triggered the vogue for wild-animal acts.

By the end of the First World War, the traditional equestrian circus had given way to new, hugely popular "star performers" on the flying trapeze. Clowns remained true to
30   their theatrical roots, however, maintaining an important role in every circus, although in America they were now confined to oversized visual gags because of the vast size and arrangement of the three-ringed circus.

In 1919, Lenin nationalised Russian circuses and many of their performers, natives of Western Europe, left the country. In response, the Soviet government established the
35   State College for Circus and Variety Arts, better known as the Moscow Circus School. This not only rejuvenated the Russian circus, it also developed training methods modelled on sports gymnastics but directed by choreographers. Innovative techniques and apparatus led to the invention of entirely new kinds of act, in which Russian performers displayed unparalleled artistry and amazing techniques.

40   Elsewhere, resistance to change had transformed tradition into routine. Old circus families hung on to what they knew, but they were rapidly losing touch in an ever-changing world. A few producers tried to modernise the staging and lighting, and add musical accompaniment. In 1974, Annie Fratellini (heiress of a famous clowning dynasty) and Alexis Gruss Jr (heir to the last French equestrian dynasty) created the
45   first two Western circus schools in Paris. Both retained a traditional approach.

This was followed in 1977 by the World Festival of the Circus of Tomorrow in Paris, set up to promote a new generation of circus performers. Based on the Gruss/Fratellini model, it quickly stimulated other experiments. In 1984, Guy Laliberté created the innovative Cirque du Soleil, a circus with an artistic director. This had a profound
50   influence on the development of a new circus movement, redefining the circus as an exciting new entertainment.

More recently, a surge of teaching activity has led to a multitude of avant-garde and experimental circus companies. Now, in the 21st century, the circus, which has always been a highly adaptable performing art, is undergoing more cosmetic changes and a
55   new expansion.

 **Activity**

Read **Text B, *A short history of the travelling circus*,** and then answer **Section A, Question 1.**

Question 1

Imagine you live in a town that is holding a festival to celebrate its history. A travelling circus company has been hired as a family entertainment. Some people in your community are not happy with this.

Write an article for your local newspaper giving your opinion on why hiring a circus is a good idea or not.

In your article you should:

- evaluate circus acts as family entertainment
- give your views on circuses based on what you have read
- say why you think modern circuses should be encouraged or not.

Base your article on what you have read, but be careful to use your own words. Address all the bullet points.

Begin your article: "The circus as an entertainment has a long history …"

Write about 250–350 words.

Up to 15 marks are available for the content of your answer, and up to 25 marks for the quality of your writing.

This copy shows how the same text can be used to identify details for two different points of view. Arguments in favour of circuses are underlined with wavy lines and arguments against are underlined with straight lines.

📖 Text B: A short history of the travelling circus

The circus as an entertainment goes back to very ancient origins. In Ancient Rome, the "circus" was a location for watching horse and chariot races, staged battles, and displays of trained animals. The travelling circus as we know it, however, started in England during the 1770s, when Philip Astley, an ex-cavalry war veteran, brought acrobatics, riding and clowning together in a ring at his riding school near Westminster Bridge in London. The equestrian performances included trick-riding, bareback acrobatics, dressage and "liberty acts", with horses running loose in the ring.

Historic origins

We've moved on from barbaric past

Cruel

During the 19th century, equestrians, male and female, were the true stars of the circus, although floor acrobats were beginning to make their mark. The best acrobats were often clowns. At this time, circus clowns were essentially mimics who could also sing, ride a horse, juggle, present trained animals, do balancing acts or tumble. An English clown called Little Wheal became famous for regularly performing a hundred consecutive somersaults, which was quite a feat then or now.

Tightrope walkers, who were the undisputed stars of travelling fairs, were among the first professional acrobats to appear in the circus ring. They adapted their acts to become one of any circus's most prized attractions: the trapeze. This began with swinging from a slack rope, then a bar was added with vertical ropes on each side. In 1859, the French gymnast, Jules Léotard presented an act at the Cirque Napoléon in Paris in which he jumped from one trapeze to another. Léotard had invented the flying trapeze, for which he became the toast of Europe, and was the originator of a costume still used today by acrobats and dancers – the leotard.

Chance to see skilled acrobats, exciting entertainment

By the close of the 19th century, railways and automobiles were replacing horses on the roads and equestrian displays were losing their supremacy to exotic animals, especially big cats. Some trained exotic animals had appeared earlier in circus history, around 1812, at the Cirque Olympique in Paris, the Franconis presented Kioumi, the first trained elephant, but it was a later combination of circus and menagerie that triggered the vogue for wild-animal acts.

Taking animals from the wild to entertain people is unacceptable

Health and safety considerations

What if they escape!

If you want to see wild animals go to a zoo or take a wildlife sightseeing trip

By the end of the First World War, the traditional equestrian circus had given way to new, hugely popular "star performers" on the flying trapeze. Clowns remained true to their theatrical roots, however, maintaining an important role in every circus, although in America they were now confined to oversized visual gags because of the vast size and arrangement of the three-ringed circus.

Clowns are a traditional part of the circus and still popular with many people

Chance for students to see real gymnastics and how choreographers work

Something to admire and celebrate

We could be paying money to see outmoded acts with no educational or entertainment value

There is a new generation of performers and acts, not like old-fashioned circuses with performing animals

"cosmetic changes" are superficial; still retains old-fashioned way of life and outdated entertainments such as clowns

Highly skilled, trained performers (not like a common fair-ground entertainment)

We don't want to see a horrific accident

Spectacle suitable for a historic celebration event

May seem like a new entertainment but based on old tradition and circus children don't get a proper education

Basic argument

Chance to support a new generation of trained performers

In 1919, Lenin nationalised Russian circuses and many of their performers, natives of Western Europe, left the country. In response, the Soviet government established the State College for Circus and Variety Arts, better known as the Moscow Circus School. This not only rejuvenated the Russian circus, it also developed training methods modelled on sports gymnastics but directed by choreographers. Innovative techniques and apparatus led to the invention of entirely new kinds of act, in which Russian performers displayed unparalleled artistry and amazing techniques.

Elsewhere, resistance to change had transformed tradition into routine. Old circus families hung on to what they knew, but they were rapidly losing touch in an ever-changing world. A few producers tried to modernise staging and lighting, and add musical accompaniment. In 1974, Annie Fratellini (heiress of a famous clowning dynasty) and Alexis Gruss Jr (heir to the last French equestrian dynasty) created the first two western circus schools in Paris. Both retained a traditional approach.

This was followed in 1977 by the World Festival of the Circus of Tomorrow in Paris, set up to promote a new generation of circus performers. Based on the Gruss/Fratellini model, it quickly stimulated other experiments. In 1984, Guy Laliberté created the innovative Cirque du Soleil, a circus with an artistic director. This had a profound influence on the development of a new circus movement, redefining the circus as an exciting new entertainment.

More recently, a surge of teaching activity has led to a multitude of avant-garde and experimental circus companies. Now, in the 21st century, the circus, which has always been a highly adaptable performing art, is undergoing more cosmetic changes and a new expansion.

Organising your points

Once you have identified the information you want to use, you need to organise your points. You could do this by using a planning frame to plan how you want to start, the topic sentences for each of your paragraphs and how you want to conclude.

Look at how a student has used a planning frame below and written an article in response to the question on page 47. You can then study the examiner comments that follow.

Introduction and thesis statement	(My opinion) title – Bring on the clowns! Circus has ancient origins and long tradition. An ideal entertainment for our local festival.
Topic sentence 1	History Our town's origins date back to Roman times and circus was part of Roman entertainment.

Example	**Roman circus** Romans watched chariot races and trained animals, people still enjoy watching highly trained animals.
Example	**Horse and dog shows** Horse shows with show-jumping and dressage and police dog displays always draw big crowds.
Transition	**Modern circus acts** We don't want to see exotic or wild animals, but the modern circus still has clowns and trapeze acts.
Topic sentence 2	**Trapeze** Trapeze artists are following an ancient tradition too.
Example	**Live entertainment/spectacle** Modern circus artists combine sports gymnastics with artistic flair for an exciting, awe-inspiring entertainment.
Example	**Performers** These performers spend years perfecting their skills and should be encouraged not ignored.
Transition	**Back to tradition of family entertainment** Modern circuses still include clowns – laugh at together.
Topic sentence 3	**Our local festival** This festival should include activities and entertainments whole families can attend together.
Example	**Clowns make people laugh – celebrate/have fun** Circus clowns are funny and good fun, and an excellent whole-family entertainment.
Example	**Alternatives – TV and pop concerts not healthy family fun** Families spend too much time apart and this entertainment will bring them together.
Conclusion	Circus acts combine tradition built on ancient origins with modern skills and artistic performances for a 21st century spectacle. Hiring a circus is a splendid idea!

 **Activity**

Question 1, Student A: Bring on the clowns!

The circus as an entertainment has a long history dating back to Roman times. Our town has a long history, dating back to Roman times and before. This makes it a very suitable entertainment for our town's festival.

Circuses are out of fashion, that is true, but there is a strong case for seeing them as a sound, safe, satisfying family entertainment again. Let's start by considering the type of entertainment a circus offers nowdays. We don't want to see lions and tigers or elephants shut in small cages then teased with whips, that's true. But we are happy to watch police dog displays and lots of people go to horse shows so we shouldn't be too hipocriteical. Many circuses nowdays don't have animals; they host amazing trapeze acts instead. Trapeze acts are exciting spectacles created by highly trained performers and even directed by choreographers like in musical shows.

Trapeze acts have ~~been~~ developed since the 19th century into gravity-defying acts with sound and music. ~~in their acts~~. It's our chance to see an exciting, awe-inspiring, live entertainment. Ask yourselves: when else are our children going to see a live performance this year with their parents? What is wrong with getting away from the television and into a Big Top and enjoy some real excitement? What is wrong with enjoying lights and music with your family, instead of watching your kids go off to watch a dodgy concert on their own?

Our town's origins date back to Roman times and circus was part of Roman entertainment. We could even locate it in the Roman part of our town. This is an ideal entertainment for our local festival. We are celebrating how our town has come into the 21st century: what better way than to celebrate than by apploauding highly skilled performers in dare-devil acts that date back to the past?

If we want to laugh and enjoy ourselves as families in a community together hiring a circus is a good idea. And don't forget the clowns – bring on the clowns! (336 words)

 Examiner comments

Overall: Student has developed the text extremely well, but regrettably strayed from the style directed. The answer reads more like a persuasive speech than an article, with over-reliance on rhetorical questions for effect.

Writing: 14/25 marks

There is some use of effective style, but this is inconsistent. Ideas are generally well sequenced and grammar is generally accurate. A range of sentence structures is used for effect. Spelling is mostly sound but lacks proofreading.

Reading: 11/15 marks

Very effective use of explicit and implicit content of the text. The response is supported by selection of relevant details and ideas from the text.

Total: 25/40 marks

Now read another student's article. It is written in the correct style, but check to see if the bullet points have been covered appropriately.

 Activity

Question 1, Student B: Bring on the clowns!

The circus as an entertainment has a long history dating back to Roman times. This is a significant fact given that our town also dates back to Roman times, and possibly earlier. A circus (in those days was a place not an event) could even have existed here. In those days, there would have been chariot races and exotic animals from distant places roaming around the arena. That's not what people want to see in this day and age, but there is an argument that the absence of a live spectacles and exciting family entertainment would not go amiss in our modern lives.

The circus that we know with tight-rope walkers and jugglers was once what happened at travelling fairs. We still have an annual fair and we still have street entertainments so I ask ~~you to consider~~ why there is so much prejudice against the circus? Health and safety concerns will prevent wild animal acts. They may of course prevent the trapeze high-wire acts as well. They are dangerous. But that's what people want to see. To see skilled, tremendously brave (or fool-hardy) performers in glamourous costumes

~~balancing on tight-ropes and~~ throwing themselves through the air. These ~~people~~ performers have spent years perfecting their acts; the acts themselves date back to the 19th century and earlier. These days there are circus schools where gymnasts train to become performers in shows directed by choreographers. Surely this is something to see and celebrate at our festival.

A modern circus is an entertainment a family can enjoy together. Whether you like or hate clowns as an adult, most children love their costumes and mad acts. A night of fun and laughter in the warm, dark atmosphere of a circus tent will be an event many of our children will remember for a long time.

We are celebrating our town's history. It's right and appropriate that part of our celebration should include an entertainment with an equally long history. Circuses have changed over the years with the people who have performed in them. A modern circus is a spectacle not to be missed. (343 words)

 QuestionRecap

Developing and structuring your own ideas

- Jot down ways to develop the text in response to the question. Examine different points of view and make a note of advantages/ disadvantages, pros/cons.
- Decide on an appropriate structure for your composition in order to deliver an effective message and conclusion. Organise your material according to the bullet points and number the points you found in the text in the order you want to include them.
- Find evidence or examples from the text to support your points, but paraphrase them in your own words

Writing your own answer

✏ **Apply**

1 Now it is your turn to answer the Directed Writing task on page 47 about hiring a travelling circus. You have already done the first stage of planning (in the Apply section on page 45), but re-read your notes and revise them if you wish.

2 Think about how you want to organise and present your argument so it leads to a sound, convincing conclusion. Carefully plan your argument using the bullet points in the question to guide you, using the planning frame below.

3 Write your article in the space on pages 53–4.

4 Re-read and edit your article. Check the word count and make any necessary changes.

Introduction and thesis statement	
Topic sentence 1	
Example	
Example	

Transition	
Topic sentence 2	
Example	
Example	
Transition	
Topic sentence 3	
Example	
Example	
Conclusion	

Activity

Question 1 (article)

....

....

....

....

....

....

....

....

(lined answer space)

[40]

(If you need more lines, write on an extra sheet of paper. Remember to write your name and the question number at the top.)

 **QuestionRecap**

Writing a letter

Planning a letter for a Directed Writing task involves three key points.

- The purpose of the letter: the purpose of this letter is to inform and discuss.
- The content: this will be based on the text.
- The reader: in this case, this is a chief councillor so the register needs to be neutral to formal and you should sign off "Yours faithfully".

Using different styles in Directed Writing

You have explored how to answer Question 1 by writing to persuade and argue in a speech and an article. Alternatively, the Directed Writing task might ask you to write a letter. A letter can discuss a subject, argue a point of view or persuade readers to your way of thinking.

✏ **Apply**

1 Read the Directed Writing task on the next page. It refers to **Text A: Seasteads for survival** on pages 38–40. Plan your answer on a planning frame like the one on pages 52–3.

2 Then write your answer in the space provided. If you need more lines use a separate sheet of paper. Remember to put your name and the number of the question, as in a real exam.

Activity

Question 1

Imagine you live in a small community very close to the coast. Your village is being threatened by rising sea levels. You read this blog article (Text A on pages 38–40) about rising sea levels and seasteads.

Write a letter to the chief councillor of your community **to discuss** whether seasteading is something the community should consider. Explain what is involved in seasteading and discuss how moving onto a floating platform or into a converted cruise ship might benefit your community.

In your letter you should:

- give your views on whether a floating village is possible
- explain how it could benefit your community
- evaluate the challenges of living out at sea.

Base your letter on what you have read in **Text A**, but be careful to use your own words. Address all the bullet points.

Begin your letter: "Dear Chief Councillor, I have been reading about seasteading …"

Write about 250–350 words.

Up to 15 marks are available for the content of your answer, and up to 25 marks for the quality of your writing.

 Link

You will find an example of a formal letter on pages 14–15 of this book.

 Activity

Question 1

....

....

....

....

....

....

....

....

....

....

....

....

....

....

....
....
....
....
....
....
....
....
....
....
....
....
....
....

[40]

(If you need more lines, write on an extra sheet of paper. Remember to write your name and the question number at the top.)

Sample Paper 2, Section B

Read the Section B questions below.

 Activity

Section B: Composition

Answer **one** question from Section B.

Write about 350–450 words on **one** of the following questions.

Up to 16 marks are available for the content and structure of your answer, and up to 24 marks for the style and accuracy of your writing.

EITHER

Descriptive Writing

2 Describe an occasion when a group of people are sharing a meal for a traditional or special celebration.

OR

Descriptive Writing

3 Describe a walk through a busy town or small village.

OR

Narrative Writing

4   Write a story that includes the words, '... they had never seen anything like it ...'.

OR

Narrative Writing

5   Write a story that involves a character who has lost something valuable.

Apply

1   Make notes in the table below about the differences between descriptive writing and narrative writing.

2   Look at the marking guidelines for descriptive and narrative compositions on page 204. Add notes to the table on what examiners are looking for in each type of composition.

	Differences	**What examiners are looking for**
Descriptive writing		
Narrative writing		

Planning your composition

Planning is a key skill in any form of writing. In Section B, it is critical because examiners will be looking at the structure of your composition as well as the content. There are 16 marks available for how well you organise your paragraphs so that they lead to a convincing conclusion. The other 24 marks are for how well you use language: your style, vocabulary and technical accuracy.

Look at how a student has made a quick mind map and wh-plan over the page for the question: Describe a walk through a busy town or small village.

Activity

Busy town

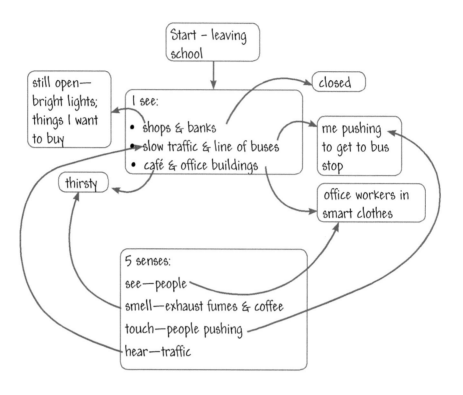

Intro

Where – my home town

When – winter evening – cold, grey, people rushing to get home from work but shops still open

Main body

Why – I'm hurrying through town to get to bus stop

Who – me, mothers with tired children, office workers in smart clothes, people rushing to get home from work but shops still open

Sense of people pushing and all going somewhere – I'm pushing through them; only traffic and line of buses (is one of them mine?) is slow

My perspective – me going home from school with heavy bag of homework BUT

tempted into brightly lit shops or a café

~~Who's waiting at bus stop?~~

Conclusion

Push on through the crowd and get to bus stop just in time

 Apply

1 Choose one of the questions on pages 56–7. Then use a mind map or spider diagram to generate ideas for your composition.

2 Link your ideas together to give an effective structure to your composition.

What examiners are looking for

There are two sample students' compositions in this section, one for Question 3 and the other for Question 5. Studying them will give you a clearer idea of what the examiners are looking for.

 Apply

1 Read each composition in turn. After you have read each one, assess it against the criteria in the table provided on page 60.

2 After you have assessed each composition, look at the examiner comments for both of them. Which is the better composition, and why?

Sample descriptive composition

 Activity

Question 3

Barnburg on a winter's day

When I was younger I used to go to Barnburg market with my grandfather who always went to the Friday market because his father was a farmer and used to sell his animals there. Barnburg market is a great place if you want to see a bit of life as it used to be in the past because it has auctions for cows and sheep and goats and hens and even horses some times.

All the aminals are in small pens and they have tickets tied on them. They're all stuffed into small pens and you can see they're stressed but and you can know it by the smell as well. I really like the sheep and goats best. The sheep have got black faces in this parts and they look funny like they've got masks on. Their wool smells special. It's got lanollin in it and some how it makes them smell warm. The goats all try to jump on top of each other to jump out of there pen. They're funny as well. The billys have got horns and you don't want to get too close to them when there all stressed out from being shut up in the pens.

As you walk through the village market you can here the auctioneer calling out really fast and loud. It sounds like gobblydyguck but when you get into the place where they have the autctions it starts to make sense. Going to the market at Barnborough used to be one of my favourite things to do I might be a farmer when I live school as well like my grandfathers father. (272 words)

Raise your marks in narrative and descriptive writing by reviewing the Glossary at www.oxfordsecondary.com/esg-for-caie-igcse or in the *Complete First Language English for Cambridge IGCSE® Student Book*. Remind yourself how to use: imagery, similes, metaphors, figurative language and emotive language.

 QuestionRecap

Good descriptive and narrative writing includes imagery using the five senses.

Link

You will find more information on writing descriptive compositions on page 23 of the *Complete First Language English for Cambridge IGCSE® Student Book*.

QuestionRecap

- Content and structure are worth 16 marks.
- Style and accuracy are worth 24 marks.
- Total = 40 marks.

Assessment of descriptive writing

How well does it:

• express what is thought, felt and imagined?	
• organise and structure ideas and opinions for effect?	
• use vocabulary and sentence structures?	
• make accurate use of spelling, punctuation and grammar?	
Opinion of the overall effect:	

Using the marking guide for Section B on page 204, decide what marks you would give this composition.

Content:	Style and accuracy:	Total marks:

 QuestionRecap

Choosing a narrator

The narrator is the person from whose point of view a descriptive or narrative composition is written. In a narrative, they recount what happened. In a description, they describe what is seen, heard, felt, tasted and smelt.

It is important to choose the right narrator because it will alter the composition. First-person narrators tell a much more personal story and show thoughts, feeling and ideas more effectively. Third-person narrators are more objective and can comment on things the characters don't know about.

Sample narrative composition

 Activity

Question 5

Lost!

She knew she knew the answer, she just couldn't find it. She looked at the exam paper and stared at the question and she remembered being in the lesson when they did this in Mr Bader's ~~lesson~~ class. She remembered doing the homework and even reading more about it in an old history book with illustrations belonging to her mother. But somehow the answer wouldn't come.

Ellie closed her eyes trying to see inside her head. She opened them and blinked and stared at the rows of heads all around her. They were all bent over their desks. Everyone was writing except her. She ~~was loosing~~ had lost her memory. She stared at the figure in front of her, a boy from another class. She looked across the isle and saw Jimmy scribbling away like his life depended on it. Which it did if you thought about it because these exams would change their lives. He'd got long black hair and it flopped over his collar on either side of his head. Some thing about his position jogged her memory. A king with long hair in a picture. A king who'd lost his crown because he wanted to rule without an elected parliament and got his head chopped off. The head over the exam paper and the head over the chopping block.

Ellie picked up her pen; it hovered over the white page. Dates, dates and actions and battles. And the outcome of those battles. Bonnie Prince Rupert, or was that someone else in another war? Then, suddenly, from empty her mind was overflowing with information. The problem now was remembering the important bits. What was important was passing this exam. She had to win this battle if only to avoid civil war at home. Her father ruled like an absolute monarch – served first at meals. The chief and only decision-maker. Some times, most times, she wasn't even a miner member of his ruling family. Her mind drifted back to a row they'd had that very morning. Her brother felt the same, too. The sooner they passed their exams and got away to college the better. Then who would Papa King rule? Words crept into her head: "The monarch is the head of the national family." Numbers floated across the blank page in front of her 1, 6, 4, 2.

That was it! She'd remembered: England 1642 the start of the Civil War when King Charles lost his country then his head. She'd remembered! She wasn't losing her memory after all. (417 words)

 Link

You will find more information on writing narrative compositions on page 75 of the *Complete First Language English for Cambridge IGCSE® Student Book.*

Assessment of narrative writing	
How well does it:	
• express what is thought, felt and imagined?	
• organise and structure ideas and opinions for effect?	
• use vocabulary and sentence structures?	
• make accurate use of spelling, punctuation and grammar?	
Opinion of the overall effect:	

Using the marking guides for Section B on page 204, decide what marks you would give this composition.

Content:	Style and accuracy:	Total marks:

Examiner comments

✓ Examiner comments

Descriptive composition

Makes a fair attempt to answer the descriptive question but too short and drifts off the task (from town/village to animal market) and into narrative style. There is some attempt to use sensory imagery (smell and sound) but vocabulary is limited and this is only partially effective. There are frequent spelling mistakes and some grammar errors. Lack of punctuation shows the composition was not checked. General lack of attention to the requirements of descriptive writing tasks.

Content and structure: 4/16 marks
Style and accuracy: 9/24 marks

Total: 13/40 marks

✓ Examiner comments

Narrative composition

Lost! shows a sophisticated approach to the narrative question. Vocabulary is not extensive and includes some well-worn phrasing ("as if his life depended on it") but otherwise it is a very skilled, controlled and effectively structured narrative showing original thought and flair. It is grammatically correct and generally error-free.

Content and structure: 16/16 marks
Style and accuracy: 21/24 marks

Total: 37/40 marks

QuestionRecap

Don't forget to write the number of the question and a title at the top.

Link

You will find more information on how to improve your narrative and descriptive writing skills on pages 78–91 of this book.

Apply

1 Return to the plans you made on page 58 and write your composition.
2 Bearing in mind what the examiners are looking for, mark your composition.

📖 Activity

Paper 2, Section B practice

....

....

....

....

....

[40]

(If you need more lines, write on an extra sheet of paper. Remember to write your name and the question number at the top.)

Review

Fill out the questionnaire below from memory.

What styles of writing do I need to know for Section A?	
What styles of writing do I need to know for Section B?	
For Section A, I need to revise …	
For Section B, I need to revise …	
For Section A, I can get help from …	
For Section B, I can get help from …	

Raise your grade

Fill out the questionnaire below to assess your progress, then make notes on what you can do to raise your grade.

	Struggling	Improve	Good
Reading skills (Section A)			
I can identify explicit meanings.			
I can identify implicit meaning (between the lines).			
I can analyse facts and opinions.			
I can develop ideas and opinions on what I have read.			
I can select and use details for a specific purpose.			
Writing skills (Sections A and B)			
I can write in different styles.			
I can change my register and tone.			
I can express what I think, feel and imagine.			
I can organise paragraphs to lead to a conclusion.			
I can spell accurately.			
I can use different sentence structures.			
I understand grammar rules.			
I can use a wide range of vocabulary.			

What I can do to raise my grade	
I can raise my marks in Section A by …	
I can raise my marks in Section B by …	
My weakest area is:	
I am fairly confident about:	
My target grade for Paper 2 is:	
I can raise my marks in Section A by …	

Objectives

In this unit you will:

- Explore what you need to include in a Coursework Portfolio
- Practise your reading skills for Assignment 1
- Explore the difference between writing to describe and narrate
- Explore what examiners are looking for
- Plan and write your own compositions
- Review your progress and how to raise your grade

Review

Component 3 – Coursework Portfolio is optional

You may take this part of the Cambridge IGCSE First Language English exam instead of Paper 2. Coursework assignments show how well you can read and develop different types of text in a Directed Writing task and how well you can write narrative and descriptive compositions.

Instead of taking Paper 2 – Writing, you may be doing Component 3, the Coursework Portfolio. Your portfolio will contain three assignments that demonstrate how well you understand the writer's craft and how well you can use language to achieve certain effects. During your course, you have developed your writing skills by reading a range of texts and responding to them in various styles for different purposes and audiences. You will use these skills for Assignment 1. You have also developed your creative writing skills to entertain and inform in narrative and descriptive compositions. You will use these skills for Assignments 2 and 3.

This unit will help you to understand the different types of assignment, the assessment objectives and what examiners are looking for in your compositiions. Work through the unit, then answer the review questions at the end to monitor your progress.

Preparing for Component 3 involves improving both your reading and writing skills so that you are more effective at:

- developing texts for Directed Writing (Assignment 1)
- planning and preparing different types of composition
- writing to discuss, argue and persuade
- writing to inform and entertain
- editing and proofreading your work.

What is included in this Coursework Portfolio

Your portfolio will contain three compositions (assignments) through which you demonstrate your reading, writing and thinking skills. Compositions may be handwritten or word-processed and printed, and you may use a dictionary.

Each of the three assignments will be about 500–800 words in length. They may be written in any order. Each piece of work will be marked on its content and style. Your portfolio is assessed first by your teacher, then by examiners.

The three pieces of work are:

- **Assignment 1:** writing to discuss, argue and/or persuade in response to a text or texts
- **Assignment 2:** writing to describe
- **Assignment 3:** writing to narrate.

You must include the first draft of one of your three assignments, although this will not contribute to your final mark for the portfolio. You must also include the text(s) you choose for Assignment 1.

Assessment objectives

Assignments 1–3 test your writing skills

You need to show how well you:

- articulate experience and express what you think, feel and imagine
- organise and structure your ideas and opinions for a deliberate effect
- use vocabulary and sentence structures appropriate to a context
- use register appropriate to the context of your topic and target reader
- spell and use punctuation and grammar correctly.

Assessment objectives

Assignment 1 also tests your reading skills

You need to show how well you:

- understand explicit meanings in a text
- understand the writer's implicit meanings and attitudes
- analyse, evaluate and develop facts, ideas and opinions, using appropriate support from the text
- select and use information for a specific purpose.

> **Exam tip**
>
> **Organising your time for Component 3**
>
> There is no time constraint, so you can take as much time and write as many drafts as you like. You are allowed to submit handwritten compositions, but consider typing them on a computer and submitting printed copies because it is easier to edit these.

Your written assignments are worth a total of 80 marks. This includes 15 marks for your reading for Assignment 1 and 65 marks for your writing in all three assignments. The portfolio is worth 50 per cent of your final grade.

Assignment 1 – Writing to discuss, argue and/or persuade

You must choose a text, or texts, and respond to it in one of the following styles: an article, a letter or the words of a speech.

The text(s) must be included in your portfolio. This will be used by your teacher and examiners to assess your reading skills.

Choosing a suitable text

You are advised to select a text or text(s) of approximately two sides of A4 in total.

Choose an interesting and informative article, blog post, letter or speech. Literature texts, stories or poems are *not* suitable for this assignment. It should contain facts, opinions and/or arguments that you can select, analyse and evaluate. The content of the text should also enable you to express your own views.

Your text can be of local, national or global interest, or all three. It can be taken from a variety of sources, such as newspapers, magazine articles, travel writing, text-based websites or blogs, but be sure to check that the source is reliable and the content is sound.

In Assignment 1, you should be able to give an overview of the whole text to show you understand the explicit meaning, then comment on specific ideas presented by the writer. Depending on the style of writing you choose (article, letter, speech), you should be able to include an explanation of interesting ideas and an argument for or against them, as well as examining the writer's argument for flaws, inconsistencies, bias and prejudice.

> **Exam tip**
>
> When you have chosen an appropriate text, take a copy of it straightaway. Make sure you record exactly where you found it and, if it is from an online newspaper, web page or blog, the date you accessed it. Then it will be ready to include in your portfolio without searching for it again. Better still, take two copies – one to work with and the other for your portfolio.

Here are some ideas on the types of text to use, how to find them and how to get started.

1 Local news report or article

Look for a report or article on a new building development or a demolition project in your local newspaper. For example, in the area in which you live or that you know well, old buildings are being pulled down to create space for a new shopping area or high-rise apartments blocks. You feel strongly about this, either because it is improving your area or because it is destroying local heritage.

Write a letter to the editor of the newspaper in which you argue for or against the proposed ideas. Evaluate the ideas and opinions presented in the report or article and centre your arguments around what is said.

2 Transcript of a speech

Find the transcript of a speech by a well-known person about an important topical issue or by a young person trying to bring about social changes. You could type "transcripts of speeches by celebrities" into your search engine to find a topic that you know something about and/or about which you feel strongly. For example, it might be a speech on charity aid or a social or environmental issue.

Write an article for a student blog or magazine arguing for or against what the person is trying to do, and saying why. You will need to evaluate the ideas and opinions presented in the speech and centre your arguments around what the person has said and/or done.

3 Travel guide

Find an article in the travel section of a daily newspaper or an online travel blog. For example, it could be a travel guide or article that you disagree with because it urges tourists to visit a protected area of outstanding natural beauty.

Write an article for a blog or newspaper on why tourists should not be encouraged to visit this area. Persuade your readers that tourism is detrimental to the area.

4 Article on popular culture

Look for an article that presents young people as thoughtless consumers only interested in music, fashion and social media. It should give you a chance to express your own ideas and opinions.

Write a speech for your school's open day on what young people can offer society today and why adults should not be prejudiced by what they read in the media.

✎ Apply

Read the following text chosen by a student and the letter she wrote in response to it. Study her notes on why the text was suitable and make your own notes on the process of choosing and annotating a text. Keep your notes for reference when you choose your own text.

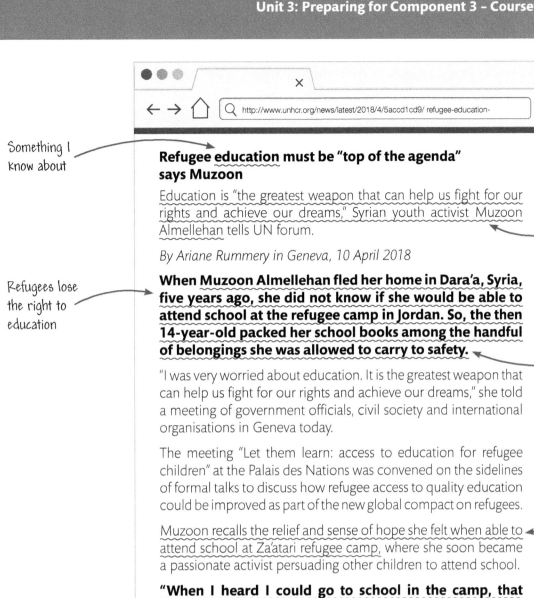

http://www.unhcr.org/news/latest/2018/4/5accd1cd9/ refugee-education-

Something I know about

Refugee education must be "top of the agenda" says Muzoon

Education is "the greatest weapon that can help us fight for our rights and achieve our dreams," Syrian youth activist Muzoon Almellehan tells UN forum.

Explain how education is a weapon against the poverty trap

By Ariane Rummery in Geneva, 10 April 2018

Refugees lose the right to education

When Muzoon Almellehan fled her home in Dara'a, Syria, five years ago, she did not know if she would be able to attend school at the refugee camp in Jordan. So, the then 14-year-old packed her school books among the handful of belongings she was allowed to carry to safety.

Emotive language

"I was very worried about education. It is the greatest weapon that can help us fight for our rights and achieve our dreams," she told a meeting of government officials, civil society and international organisations in Geneva today.

The meeting "Let them learn: access to education for refugee children" at the Palais des Nations was convened on the sidelines of formal talks to discuss how refugee access to quality education could be improved as part of the new global compact on refugees.

Muzoon recalls the relief and sense of hope she felt when able to attend school at Za'atari refugee camp, where she soon became a passionate activist persuading other children to attend school.

Hope for a better future/a good job means a safer future (implicit meanings)

Use quote as an emotive appeal

"When I heard I could go to school in the camp, that moment changed my life."

"When I heard I could go to school in the camp, that moment changed my life. It gave me hope and made me stronger. It made me who I am now," said Muzoon, now 20, who has since moved to the United Kingdom with her family and become UNICEF's youngest goodwill ambassador.

There is a deeper issue. Not all children get even a basic education (we are lucky and should do what we can to help)

This is a worldwide problem but we can begin to help the situation in our own community

"I am so lucky now I live in the UK with my family. But I cannot be completely happy without seeing every child in the world with access to quality education. I am fighting for every child, not just refugees, for every child over the world."

Muzoon has a strong plea for governments around the world meeting in Geneva this week as part of formal consultations on the refugee compact, and calls on them to put education at the "top of the agenda."

Explain why students should be aware that universal education should be top of the agenda

Help refugees in our area and lobby for better conditions in refugee camps elsewhere

The compact aims to transform the way the international community responds to refugee crises, and in particular to find ways for refugees to be better included in host communities which in turn should receive more robust and reliable support.

Other speakers at today's meeting called on governments to ensure access to quality and timely education opportunities for refugee children and youth, who fall far behind their peers.

What happens to young people who cannot go to school and/or get professional skills or further education?

Worldwide, only 61% of refugee children attend primary school compared with the global rate of 91% according to a UNHCR study. Even fewer, 23% refugee children, attend secondary school compared to a global rate of 84%. Only one per cent of refugee youth attend university compared to 36% of youth globally.

"The vast majority of refugee children face the double jeopardy of losing their homes and their education," said Joseph Nhan-O'Reilly, Head of Education Policy and Advocacy at Save the Children.

"Quality education is really the be all and end all of everything."

He noted refugees can face particular challenges and called for the compact to detail practical actions that will "move the needle in closing the education gap," making a tangible difference for refugee children.

The meeting heard that proper technical and financial support was needed for hosting governments so they can include refugees in their national education sector plans. Refugees may also need bridging programmes or intensive language support in order to transition to local schools.

Summing up today's meeting, UNHCR's Assistant High Commission for Protection, Volker Türk, noted: "Quality education is really the be all and end all of everything. It helps protect refugee children, giving them hope in their future, and promotes social cohesion. Investments in education can also provide real opportunities for host communities."

UNHCR was given the task of developing a global compact on refugees by the UN General Assembly in this historic New York Declaration for Refugees and Migrants of 19 September 2016, in which 193 governments pledged to forge a fairer global system. Formal consultations are currently underway, and the compact is expected to be adopted by UN Member States at the end of 2018.

Source: From the United Nations High Commission for Refugees Website: http://www.unhcr.org/news/latest/2018/4/5accd1cd9/refugee-education-must-top-agenda-says-muzoon.html accessed 17/05/18

Annotations:

Frightening statistic

So refugees cannot become doctors, engineers, scientists and help their own people in the long term

Use this quote

Must ensure refugees are better cared for in host communities, leading to better understanding of their situation and more acceptance by local people

Sum up speech using this to reinforce argument

725 words – the right length – approximately 2 sides of A4

A UN programme to protect refugees, a reliable source

Show where text comes from and when it was accessed

Why this is a suitable text

It contains:

- a topic I know about (education)
- a situation that is currently in the news
- something many people overlook or try to avoid
- something meaningful for our future
- something I feel strongly about
- explicit meanings
- implicit meanings (what happens to uneducated children of refugees)
- a global issue (education)
- data and statistics to support my argument
- emotive language.

My response: a letter to our school principal persuading him to let me speak about this in our school assembly, and what I want my fellow students to do.

 QuestionRecap

Writing to argue and persuade presents a case and promotes the writer's point of view. This style of writing needs to be logical and convincing.

Other possible responses to this text

This text contains both explicit content and implicit meanings that could be developed in various ways. For example, it could also be used in:

- a persuasive speech on why more should be done to help refugees in the local area
- a speech to persuade people to support refugees on a global scale
- a letter to the editor of a local newspaper showing why refugee children should be admitted to local schools
- an article for a school magazine on why young people should invest in their future through education
- a feature article for a newspaper calling for politicians to grant more funds for refugees and especially for the education of refugee children
- an article on the problems facing refugees in camps around the world.

 Link

You will find more on writing letters, articles and speeches in Unit 2 of this book. There is information about writing to discuss, argue and persuade throughout the *Complete First Language English for Cambridge IGCSE® Student Book* and you will find more on writing a persuasive speech on pages 144–45 of the *Complete First Language English for Cambridge IGCSE® Student Book*.

 Apply

1 How would you use the text on refugee education? Choose a way to respond (discuss/argue/persuade) and a suitable form of writing (letter/article/speech).
2 Make notes here on how you would respond to this text and why.

....

....

....

....

....

....

....

....

 QuestionRecap

You also have to include the first draft of one of your compositions in your portfolio.

Planning to write Assignment 1

The next stage is to start planning your composition – a key stage in writing any coursework assignment.

 Apply

1 Here are some different planning strategies. Can you add to the list?

- mind maps
- spider diagrams
- topic sentence lists
- writing frames

2 Think about how you choose and/or combine planning strategies. Which type of plan would you prefer to use for the following writing styles?

Writing style	Planning strategy
Writing to discuss, argue and/or persuade	
Writing to entertain in narrative compositions	
Writing to entertain in descriptive compositions	

 Link

There is more advice on writing to argue and persuade on page 39 of the *Complete First Language English for Cambridge IGCSE® Student Book*.

◀◀ **QuestionRecap**

Planning a composition to argue and persuade

- Examine the topic carefully from different points of view, both for and against.
- Decide on your standpoint and prepare your argument.
- Number the points in the order you want to make them. Will you give all the arguments in favour first, then arguments against second, or will you alternate them?
- Use a suitable planning strategy to plan your composition.
- Make sure you can support your point of view with evidence from the text.

Look at how the same student has used mind mapping to start planning her response to the article about refugees on pages 69–70.

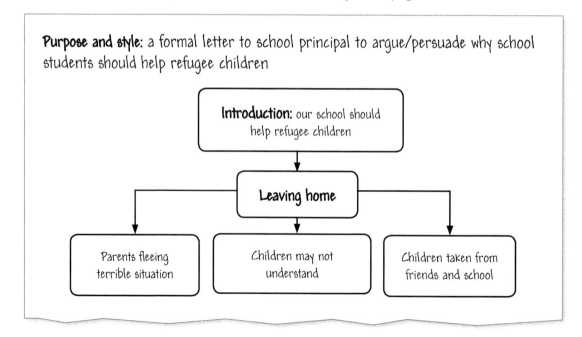

Purpose and style: a formal letter to school principal to argue/persuade why school students should help refugee children

Introduction: our school should help refugee children

Leaving home

Parents fleeing terrible situation

Children may not understand

Children taken from friends and school

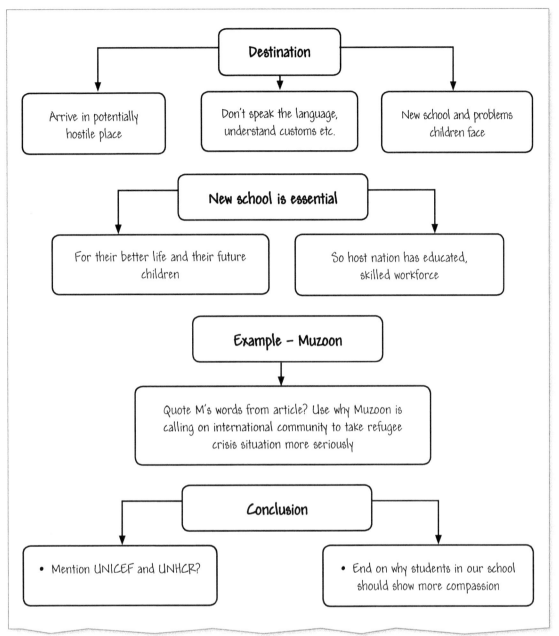

Introduction	Reason for writing (persuade principal to encourage students to take action)
Paragraph 1	Who are refugees and why they leave their home countries
Paragraph 2	What happens to refugee children in our school
Paragraph 3	Case of Muzoon – what Muzoon is asking for and why
Paragraph 4	How we can help – older students partnering new students
Conclusion	We need a change in social thinking – have more compassion for refugees

 Link

For more ideas on writing frames to help you to organise your thoughts and plan paragraphs, see pages 49–50 in this book.

 **QuestionRecap**

Topic sentences

When planning a composition to argue and persuade, it is useful to plan a topic sentence to start or be included in each paragraph.

- The introduction (thesis statement) should state your case.
- Each topic sentence must be relevant and further your argument.
- The final topic sentence should link back to the thesis statement and/or the opening of your composition.

QuestionRecap

You will find more on Directed Writing techniques and strategies in Unit 2.

What the examiners are looking for

✎ Apply

1 Read the student's composition below, then mark it using the marking guide for Assignment 1 on page 205. Comment on:

Content and use of the original text (reading skills)	
Style and register (writing skills)	
Spelling, punctuation and grammar (technical accuracy)	

2 Then read the examiner comments which follow.

Assignment 1

A letter to a school principal in response to a UNHCR article on refugee education

(http://www.unhcr.org/news/latest/2018/4/5accd1cd9/refugee-education-must-top-agenda-says-muzoon. html, accessed 17/05/18)

Dear Principal,

In the past few months there have been some new pupils in our school, but I am afraid we are not doing much to help them. These pupils have travelled long distances, they do not know our language or our customs, and they need our help. It is my belief we can and should help them to integrate into our school life and local community better, this in turn will help their families. As a school we can do a lot to not just help our new pupils but change people's attitudes to refugees in general.

Leaving your home and all you know and love to live in another country is difficult: how much more difficult must it be when you are forced from your home, knowing you will probably never return – and that you are not wanted anywhere? This is probably why our new pupils cling together at break time and after school. They feel they have no friends, which is perhaps natural but very sad, and something we can remedy.

At present, we are not encouraging them sufficiently to learn our language or to be part of our community. I think our school should take active steps to improve their situation. A recent article on the UNHCR website about refugee education has made me think a lot about this and with your permission I would like to speak about it in our weekly assembly.

Most refugee families are fleeing terrible destruction or famine in their home countries. The lucky ones finally arrive in a completely alien city or country, where they have no home and no welcome. There is a big attitude problem here, which I believe young people can do a lot to change.

In our country many refugee children are able to come to school, but this is not the case for all of them. If we, as a school and individual students, have a more positive attitude this will influence our families, who as adults can do more to help. This is vital in my opinion because both refugees and their host countries face a long-term problem if refugee children are not educated and integrated into their new environments.

According to the UNHCR study, fewer than 23% of refugee children attend secondary school, and only 1% go on to university. Without better education these children will become adults caught in the poverty trap. Having no qualifications means they will not get good jobs. This means they could be unemployed and then they are a burden on our society. This worsens the prejudice against them.

To help people in our area I would like to suggest that older students from our school 'partner' with new arrivals to help them with their homework and social life. I am motivated by reading about a Syrian youth activist called Muzoon Alemellehan, who had to leave her home when she was 14, but because she was able to get a good education later has become the UN's youngest goodwill ambassador and is now helping to alert everyone to the need for schools in refugee camps. Muzoon is doing what she can to transform the way refugees are viewed and treated on an international scale. I think that we can do a lot, too, on a local scale.

If we can help our local refugee community we will be doing them a great service, and also helping our country too. Educating refugee children will provide them with the academic skills to fight for their rights in their native countries and make it possible for them to get good jobs here if they cannot ever return. Encouraging our families to have a more positive attitude to foreign newcomers will help our local community in many ways as well.

The United Nations Children's Fund and the United Nations Human Rights Council are doing what they can at a global and international level. But we need to do more at a local level – even within this school. We need a change in social thinking so there is more compassion for refugees. They need our help, and I think our school has a lot to offer at a personal and local level. If you would allow me to speak about this in assembly I would be very grateful.

Yours sincerely,

Juana De Motte

(715 words)

 Examiner comments

Reading: 15/15 marks

Student evaluates the explicit content of the text and has a well-reasoned response to implicit ideas and opinions. Includes points and ideas from the text effectively to produce a well-developed response.

Writing: 14/15 marks

This is a very competent and effective composition in the form of a formal letter. The style conveys meanings clearly, with some subtleties. The letter is structured efficiently and leads to an effective and appropriate conclusion for the student's purpose (to argue a case and influence the reader), although this could have been improved. There is a good range of vocabulary, albeit with a few repetitions ("help"), sentence structures are varied and punctuation is correct. It uses the correct register for the reader (school principal).

Total: 29/30 marks

Writing your own composition

 Apply

1 Use the article about refugee education on pages 69–70 to write the words of a speech. You do not have to be in agreement with the student who wrote the letter – you can take a completely different approach – but you must base your writing on what is in the original text.

   a Plan your speech carefully.

   b Write a rough draft, then at least two further drafts to get the best results.

   c Check the number of words and make adjustments if necessary. Proofread and edit your composition.

   d Prepare a final copy of your composition, then give it a final check.

2 When you have finished and you are satisfied with your speech, mark it against the marking guide for Component 3 Assignment 1 on page 205.

 QuestionRecap

Your composition should be 500–800 words long and you may use a word-processor and dictionary.

QuestionRecap

Writing a composition to argue and persuade

- For each main point in your argument, start a new paragraph, with a clear topic sentence.
- Your topic sentences should lead up to and justify your conclusion.
- Support your point of view by using evidence from the text.
- If appropriate, use emotive language to persuade your readers.
- Be careful of using rhetorical questions that could get the wrong answer.

Assignment 1

....

....

....

....

....

....

....

....

....

....

(If you run out of space to plan and write your speech, continue on a new sheet of paper.)

Raising your grade for Assignment 1

The most effective way to raise your grade for Assignment 1 is to become a perfectionist.

- Draft and redraft your composition as many times as you need to.
- Use a thesaurus to find alternative ways to say something if you discover unintended repetitions.
- Spend time thinking about the content and structure of your argument. Play around with the organisation and structure of your paragraphs to lead to the conclusion.
- Check and double check your spelling and grammar to be sure you have no weak areas that will bring down your marks.
- Do not submit your assignment until you are sure you cannot improve it.

Assignment 2 – Writing to describe

Writing to describe is an excellent opportunity to demonstrate your creative writing skills. Show your understanding of the writer's craft through your use of figurative language and different forms of imagery.

Choosing what to write about

Choose a topic that enables you to demonstrate your writing skills, especially those related to personal observations, thoughts and feelings. Descriptive compositions are more convincing if they contain material you know about from personal experience. It is not necessary for you to have experienced exactly the same situation, but you should be able to depict it well because you have experienced something similar.

You may submit poetry for Assignment 2, but each poem must be accompanied by a commentary or explanation on how it came to be written. This will be included in the word count.

Link

You will find more on writing to describe in Unit 2 of this book.

Exam tip

Remember not to turn descriptive writing into a story.

Apply

Below are some ideas to help you find a suitable topic for this assignment. Adapt, change and/or add to them to suit your personality and style of writing.

Places
- You are in a dental surgery, waiting for your appointment. Describe your surroundings and your thoughts and feelings as you wait.
- You have taken your pet to a veterinary practice. Describe your surroundings, including the people and animals you can see.
- Choose a busy place that provides a definite sense of location and has a particular atmosphere, e.g. a café, an underground train station, an airport or a sports stadium. This will give you a range of sights, smells and sounds, and people to describe.
- My idea(s):

....

....

Occasions
- Describe an important gathering or celebration. This should be a time or event that provides a definite sense of place/atmosphere and contains a range of sights, sounds and/or characters to comment on and/or describe in more detail.
- Choose a traditional event that your family and/or friends celebrate or that you have witnessed. It should give you the opportunity to discuss food (taste), costumes (colour and texture), music or noise (sound).
- My idea(s):

....

....

What examiners are looking for

A good way to pick up marks in Assignment 2 is to use figurative and more literary language. Remember to use imagery involving the five senses so your reader can really appreciate what you are describing.

 **QuestionRecap**

Recap on figurative language and different forms of imagery by referring to the Glossary at www.oxfordsecondary.com/ esg-for-caie-igcse.

✎ Apply

1 Read the descriptive composition below and make notes on what you think is good or not so good about it. You can annotate the text, but then write your overall assessment here. What are its strengths and weaknesses?

....

....

....

....

....

2 Turn to page 206 and look at the marking guidelines for Assignment 2. What marks would you give this composition? Write in your marks and your reasons for awarding them.

Content and structure: **10 marks are available**	
Style and accuracy: **15 marks are available**	

3 Then look at how an examiner marked it on pages 81–82.

Assignment 2
Hang-gliding

I have only been hang-gliding once, but it was an unforgettable experience. To start with, when they told me we were going hang-gliding for my birthday treat I thought "some treat!" It wasn't what I would have chosen – ever.

Later, when I met Sebastian, who was leading the expedition up the mountain, I was even more doubtful. Sebastian is a large mountain-man. That is, he has a broad chest, an equally broad back and long, strong legs, which make him perfectly equipped to stride up the grassy areas and scramble over the rocky outcrops to get to the area where they "jump". I can tell you all this because I had plenty of time to study his back and movements as I tried to keep up with him for many, many metres above sea level.

 Link

There is more on the assessment of descriptive writing for Component 3 and Paper 2 on page 23 of the *Complete First Language English for Cambridge IGCSE® Student Book*.

This, I should explain, was part of my problem. I live at sea-level. I am not accustomed to hiking at altitude. I am a school pupil who only runs when I can't get out of it in Physical Education lessons, and never goes on any form of hike. The point I'm trying to explain is that I am not fit. Add this to the fact that I'm not good with heights either and you have a good idea about how I was feeling the morning we hiked up a French mountain so we could jump off it with a pair of plastic wings. In the end, there weren't even any wings – just a multi-coloured hood.

Eventually, we did get to the place where they "jump". I tried to pretend that word didn't matter. To be honest, I was so exhausted when we finally got to the hang-gliders' launch pad they could have told me to "dive" off it and I probably would have done.

Then, quite suddenly, I was in some sort of harness, wearing some sort of helmet two sizes too big. Sebastian told me to run. I ran. Into thin air. Then I wasn't running, I was floating in the air. To say it takes your breath away is an understatement: it is the most magical experience.

Sebastian, who had the controls, managed to make us rise and we were flying along the edge of a cliff with eagles. There's a silence in the air, but it is not any sort or silence that I could describe because with this silence there is the faintest of hushing, rushing, gently-whining sound. Perhaps it was the effect of the wings, I don't know, but I will remember it for ever. It was broken by another noise that pierced my soul. The scream of an eagle at close distance. We were straying too near her nest. My heart missed at least two beats, then it settled back to its normal rhythm and I took stock of what was happening below.

Below, far, far below small people moved across a meadow like mice. Cars like coloured wagons made their way across the opposite side of the valley. An old-fashioned motor coach clanged its horn like a toy.

A river ran silver as a summer trout into the valley and I could see how humans had made their mark on what was once a pristine environment. The thought ran through my head that this one experience would change me.

It has. I vaguely remember coming down to the meadow to land, and how my legs were wobbly. The hang-glider came down in wide turns, just as eagles do. In a moment my feet touched springy tussocks of grass, I nearly tripped but didn't and ran as I was instructed to get out from under the parachute device. It was all over. But my head was still, literally, in the clouds.

I don't remember anything else about that day. My head was full of the way eagles glide and call to each other; how water falls from a crevice in rocks to form a stream and join a river. It was magical and life-changing.

(664 words)

Activity

Assignment 2
Hang-gliding

I have only been hang-gliding once, but it was an unforgettable experience. To start with, when they told me we were going hang-gliding for my birthday treat I thought "some treat!". It wasn't what I would have chosen – ever.

Falls into story frame

Correct use of punctuation

Later, when I met Sebastian, who was leading the expedition up the mountain, I was even more doubtful. Sebastian is a large mountain-man. That is, he has a broad chest, an equally broad back and long, strong legs, which make him perfectly equipped to stride up the grassy areas and scramble over the rocky outcrops to get to the area where they "jump". I can tell you all this because I had plenty of time to study his back and movements as I tried to keep up with him for many, many metres above sea level.

Check this doesn't become a narrative

This, I should explain, was part of my problem. I live at sea-level. I am not accustomed to hiking at altitude. I am a school pupil who only runs when I can't get out of it in Physical Education lessons, and never goes on any form of hike. The point I'm trying to explain is that I am not fit. Add this to the fact that I'm not good with heights either and you have a good idea about how I was feeling the morning we hiked up a French mountain so we could jump off it with a pair of plastic wings. In the end, there weren't even any wings – just a multi-coloured hood.

Humour and bathos

Eventually we did get to the place where they "jump". I tried to pretend that word didn't matter. To be honest I was so exhausted when we finally got to the hang-gliders' launch pad they could have told me to "dive" off it and I probably would have done.

Figurative language for humorous effect

Then, quite suddenly, I was in some sort of harness, wearing some sort of helmet two sizes too big. Sebastian told me to run. I ran. Into thin air. Then I wasn't running, I was floating in the air. To say it takes your breath away is an understatement: it is the most magical experience.

Effective use of simple and minor sentences

Good punctuation

Sebastian, who had the controls, managed to make us rise and we were flying along the edge of a cliff with eagles. There's a silence in the air, but it is not any sort or silence that I could describe because with this silence there is the faintest of hushing, rushing, gently-whining sound. Perhaps it was the effect of the wings, I don't know, but I will remember it for ever. It was broken by another noise that pierced my soul. The scream of an eagle at close distance. We were straying too near her nest. My heart missed at least two beats, then it settled back to its normal rhythm and I took stock of what was happening below.

Aural imagery

Good use of language

Changes tenses, then slips back to past tense – showing how this memory has stayed with him? Change of tone to convey experience

Good use of poetic language

Below, far, far below, small people moved across a meadow like mice. Cars like coloured wagons made their way across the opposite side of the valley. An old-fashioned motor coach clanged its horn like a toy.

Similes here

A river ran silver as a summer trout into the valley and I could see how humans had made their mark on what was once a pristine environment. The thought ran through my head that this one experience would change me.

Articulates experience

It has. I vaguely remember coming down to the meadow to land and how my legs were wobbly. The hang-glider came down in wide turns, just as eagles do. In a moment my feet touched springy tussocks of grass, I nearly tripped but didn't and ran as I was instructed to get out from under the parachute device. It was all over. But my head was still, literally, in the clouds.

Tactile imagery

Check this doesn't become a narrative

I don't remember anything else about that day. My head was full of the way eagles glide and call to each other; how water falls from a crevice in rocks to form a stream and join a river. It was magical and life-changing.

Articulates experience

(664 words)

Examiner comments

General comments

Student expresses what he thinks, feels and imagines during a hang-gliding experience. This is articulated well with a conscious change in style and mood halfway through to show how he reacted to being in a hang-glider. This is a very competent, enjoyable piece of writing despite a few technical flaws.

Content and structure: 10/10 marks

Complex, engaging and effective content with structure organised for a specific effect.

Well-defined and well-chosen images create a convincing picture with varieties of focus.

Style and accuracy: 14/15 marks

Very satisfactory use of vocabulary and figurative language. There are some minor limitations. Uses varied sentence structures. Handles register well, changing tone for effect during the composition. Spelling, punctuation and grammar almost always accurate.

Total: 24/25 marks

Planning to write Assignment 2

 Apply

Choose a topic from page 78 – either a place or an occasion – and plan a descriptive composition on the next page. What is the best type of planning strategy for your chosen composition?

 QuestionRecap

Keep in mind that you have to write 500–800 words.

Assignment 2 – plan

 QuestionRecap

Mood and tone

These are important features of descriptive and narrative compositions. The words and images a writer chooses contribute to how the reader perceives the atmosphere of a scene. Mood and tone are created through a combination of:

- diction (word choice)
- rhythm of the language (pace)
- use of imagery
- sound effects created through alliteration, assonance and/or sibilance.

Writing your own composition

 Apply

1 Before you start to write, think about your point of view and the mood and tone you want to achieve in your composition.

2 Write the first draft of your composition in the space below.

3 Refer to the marking guidelines on page 206 at the back of the book and decide how you can improve your composition. Annotate your first draft with your ideas for improvement.

Link

You can find more on point of view, mood and tone in Unit 3 of the *Complete First Language English for Cambridge IGCSE® Student Book*.

Assignment 2: first draft

....
....
....
....
....
....
....

....

....

....

....

....

....

....

....

....

....

....

....

....

....

....

....

....

....

....

....

(If you run out of space to write your draft, continue on a new sheet of paper.)

Raising your grade for Assignment 2

The most effective way to raise your grade for Assignment 2 is to become a perfectionist.

- Draft and redraft your composition as many times as you need to.
- Use a thesaurus to find alternative ways to say something if you discover unintended repetitions.
- Flick through the Glossary at www.oxfordsecondary.com/esg-for-caie-igcse to remind yourself of ways to use figurative language.
- Play around with words and sentence structures to convey your chosen mood or tone.
- Check and double check your spelling and grammar to be sure you have no weak areas that will bring down your marks.
- Do not submit your assignment until you are sure you cannot improve it.

Assignment 3 – Writing to narrate

This assignment calls for narrative writing, which you can write in any narrative form: in the first or third person, past or present tense, and any style or genre.

You need to develop a meaningful and well-defined plot or storyline, include complex characters and create realistic dialogue. The narrative and details need to be convincing: you want your reader to suspend disbelief and "live" your story.

Choosing what to write about

Narrative compositions are more convincing if they contain material you know about from personal experience. It is not necessary for you to have experienced exactly the same situation, but you should be able to depict it well because you have felt similar emotions or been in similar circumstances.

If you are not very confident about writing a short story with a clear beginning, middle and an end, consider writing a journal entry or something from an older person's memoir. You could also write diary entries for three different days that form a story when put together.

✐ **Apply**

Below are some ideas to help you find a suitable topic for this assignment. Jot down your own ideas here.

....

....

....

....

....

....

....

Ideas for Assignment 3
- Set yourself a challenge: choose some words that have to fit into your story such as "Then they realised they were the only ones there ..."
- A fictional coming-of-age account of a life-changing event
- An autobiographical account of being accused of something that you did not do or when you are obliged to tell the truth against your will
- A short story that involves a comic hero or a superhero such as Batman or Wonderwoman
- A story involving a character from a film or television series; your story provides "backstory" for the screen version
- An updated retelling of a legend, such as a first-person account of Beowulf, or a folktale about a modern Cinderella
- A domestic comedy or tragedy about what happens when your family car is trapped in a huge traffic jam for hours

Link

You will find more on Narrative Writing in Unit 2 on pages 60–1; on how fiction authors use narrators and the narrative voice on page 181 of the *Complete First Language English for Cambridge IGCSE® Student Book*; and on showing and telling in a short story in Unit 7 of the *Complete First Language English for Cambridge IGCSE® Student Book*.

 **QuestionRecap**

Showing and telling in a short story

An omniscient third-person narrator tells a story using two techniques – show and tell.

- They show us people's characters through what they say, how they speak and how they react to one another. We can also learn about the past and the future from what characters say.
- The narrator tells us about the characters through description and setting, including what characters look like, where they are and what is happening to them.

An omniscient narrator knows what all the characters are thinking. Thoughts are conveyed by the narrator:

- showing what a character is thinking through free indirect thought (e.g. Is it over yet?)
- telling us what a character is thinking through direct thought (e.g. "Is it over yet," he wondered.).

What examiners are looking for

A good way to pick up marks in Assignment 3 is to choose an appropriate narrative voice.

Apply

1 Read the narrative composition on the next page and make notes on what you think is good or not so good about it. You can annotate the text, but then write your overall assessment here. What are its strengths and weaknesses?

....

....

....

....

....

2 Turn to page 206 and look at the marking guidelines for Assignment 3. What marks would you give this composition? Write in your marks and your reasons for awarding them.

Content and structure: 10 marks are available	
Style and accuracy: 15 marks are available	

3 Then look at how an examiner marked it on pages 88–9.

Assignment 3

The Visit

The queue to see the art museum went round the block. It seemed to Gemma that there were more tourists in this city than inhabitants. She used her day itinerary to fan herself and looked longingly at the café opposite. A nice long drink and a morning sitting watching what was going would be so much nicer than another visit to another museum.

"Oh look!" Monica cried.

A small, black and white dog had got loose in the café terrace opposite the museum and was running in and out of people's legs. Two children were running after it squealing at each other and the dog. A man stamped down on the poor creature's lead and it was yanked back to a stop.

"Poor thing," Gemma muttered. "What's she saying now?" Gemma was referring to Miss Pinkerton their art teacher.

"... each painting tells a story in this gallery. Look into each one and try to see what the artist is telling you. This is not conceptual art, like we saw yesterday, this is –"

Gemma stopped listening. The queue shuffled forward and they started going into the cool, dark interior. As soon as she could, Gemma separated herself from her classmates and started looking for somewhere to sit down. There was an inviting bench placed in front of a vast painting. She headed straight for it.

The music in her headphones was calming. Sibelius: her secret. She never told anyone, they'd laugh. Without doing it very consciously, Gemma started to look into the big painting in front of her. The frame was very ornate. There were apples and oranges and flowers carved into it. Someone had taken a lot of time and trouble to make that frame. She turned her attention to the picture.

It was a street scene. Somewhere in old Spain perhaps judging by the orange trees and the white houses. A woman in a tight black bodice and long blue skirt was running towards her. Apples were falling out of her basket. An old woman was scuttling into a doorway. A street vendor with a cart was leaving his goods to get to safety. A boy and girl had jumped behind a table that had fallen over. Behind them, head down, came a big brown bull. Running alongside it was a small black and white dog. Gemma could hear it yapping. She knew that dog from somewhere. Then she could hear the bull's heavy breathing. It thundered towards her. Horns a metre long lowered to lift her into the air – or worse. She threw herself off the bench to get out of its way.

"Gemma! What are doing?" snapped Miss Pink.

Gemma looked up from behind the bench. "The bull," she gulped, "it got loose, I was ..."

"You were what? Trying to escape it?" Miss Pink's voice held a sneer. Gemma got to her feet. "And you can give me those ear-phone things, please." She held out her hand and Gemma handed over her smart phone. "And now pay more attention to the paintings, please. This is why we are here, is it not? Each of these paintings, as I told you earlier, tell a story. I shall be asking you later what you have learned from them."

"Yes, Miss Pink," Gemma replied, trying not to smile.

(553 words)

Activity

Limited use of vocabulary but interesting observation on tourists and the downside of school trips

Assignment 3
The Visit

The queue to see the art museum went round the block. It seemed to Gemma that there were more tourists in this city than inhabitants. She used her day itinerary to fan herself and looked longingly at the café opposite. A nice long drink and a morning sitting watching what was going would be so much nicer than another visit to another museum.

"Oh look!" Monica cried.

A small, black and white dog had got loose in the café terrace opposite the museum and was running in and out of people's legs. Two children were running after it squealing at each other and the dog. A man stamped down on the poor creature's lead and it was yanked back to a stop.

"Poor thing," Gemma muttered. "What's she saying now?" Gemma was referring to Miss Pinkerton their art teacher.

"... each painting tells a story in this gallery. Look into each one and try to see what the artist is telling you. This is not conceptual art, like we saw yesterday, this is –"

Gemma stopped listening. The queue shuffled forward and they started going into the cool, dark interior. As soon as she could, Gemma separated herself from her classmates and started looking for somewhere to sit down. There was an inviting bench placed in front of a vast painting. She headed straight for it.

The music in her headphones was calming. Sibelius: her secret. She never told anyone, they'd laugh. Without doing it very consciously, Gemma started to look into the big painting in front of her. The frame was very ornate. There were apples and oranges and flowers carved into it. Someone had taken a lot of time and trouble to make that frame. She turned her attention to the picture.

It was a street scene. Somewhere in old Spain perhaps judging by the orange trees and the white houses. A woman in a tight black bodice and long blue skirt was running towards her. Apples were falling out of her basket. An old woman was scuttling into a doorway. A street vendor with a cart was leaving his goods to get to safety. A boy and girl had jumped behind a table that had fallen over. Behind them, head down, came a big brown bull. Running alongside it was a small black and white dog. Gemma could hear it yapping. She knew that dog from somewhere. Then she could hear the bull's heavy breathing. It thundered towards her. Horns a metre long lowered to lift her into the air – or worse. She threw herself off the bench to get out of its way.

"Gemma! What are doing?" snapped Miss Pink.

Gemma looked up from behind the bench. "The bull," she gulped, "it got loose, I was ..."

Grammar sound, vocabulary ("nice") weaker

Good use of punctuation in dialogue

✔

✔

Good use of vocabulary – conveys action well

Correct use of past perfect

> "You were what? Trying to escape it?" Miss Pink's voice held a sneer. Gemma got to her feet. "And you can give me those ear-phone things, please." She held out her hand and Gemma handed over her smart phone. "And now pay more attention to the paintings, please. This is why we are here, is it not? Each of these paintings, as I told you earlier, tell a story. I shall be asking you later what you have learned from them."
>
> "Yes, Miss Pink," Gemma replied, trying not to smile.
>
> (553 words)

Good use of vocabulary...

... But not so good here

 Examiner comments

General comments

Student uses close third-person interior monologue and indirect thought to express what is thought, felt and imagined very well. Characters are introduced without description, but personalities are conveyed through inner thoughts and dialogue with a degree of sophistication. The plot device is neatly handled. A very competent, enjoyable piece of writing.

Content and structure: 10/10 marks

Story is simple but effective. The main character is established, the teacher given a humourless personality. The disconnect between teacher and pupil is evident. The apparently simple device of seeing the same thing twice (the small dog) and doing what one is told are given a pleasing twist.

Style and accuracy: 13/15 marks

There are some inconsistencies with repetition of basic vocabulary intermixed with more sophisticated use of words. Includes minor punctuation omissions but dialogue is handled very well. A final draft might have corrected repetitions, but otherwise good use of language.

Total: 23/25 marks

Planning and writing Assignment 3

 Apply

1 Choose a topic from page 85 or an idea of your own. Then plan your narrative composition in the space on page 90.
2 Write your composition on a separate sheet of paper.
3 Refer to the marking guidelines on page 206 and decide how you can improve your composition. Annotate your first draft with your ideas for improvement.
4 Complete as many drafts as you need to, then write up your final composition. Check and recheck it until you are sure it is as good as it can be.

 QuestionRecap

Keep in mind that you have to write 500–800 words.

 Link

Look back at page 72 to see suggested planning strategies.

My planning

Raising your grade for Assignment 3

The most effective way to raise your grade for Assignment 3 is to become a perfectionist.

- Draft and redraft your composition as many times as you need to.
- Use a thesaurus to find alternative ways to say something if you discover unintended repetitions.
- Check and double check your spelling and grammar to be sure you have no weak areas that will bring down your marks.
- Do not submit your assignment until you are sure you cannot improve it.

Exam tip

Submitting a first draft

You have to submit a first draft of one of the compositions in your portfolio, so choose one that demonstrates your editing skills.

Review

Fill out the questionnaire below from memory.

Assignment 1 is …	
In Assignment 1, I have to write in one of these styles …	
The text for my response should be about …	
Assignment 1 must include …	
In Assignment 1, these skills will be assessed …	
Assignment 2 is …	
If I write poems, I must include …	
In Assignment 2, these skills will be assessed …	
Assignment 3 is …	
In Assignment 3, my composition should include …	
In Assignment 3, these skills will be assessed …	

Raise your grade

Fill out the questionnaire below to assess your progress, then make notes on what you can do to raise your grade.

	Struggling	Improve	Good
Reading skills (Assignment 1)			
I can identify explicit meanings.			
I can identify implicit meaning (read between the lines).			
I can analyse facts and opinions.			
I can develop ideas and opinions on what I have read.			
I can select and use details for a specific purpose.			
Writing skills (Assignments 1, 2 and 3)			
I can write in different styles.			
I can change my register and tone.			
I can express what I think, feel and imagine.			
I can organise paragraphs to lead to a conclusion.			
I can spell accurately.			
I can use different sentence structures.			
I understand grammar rules.			
I can use a wide range of vocabulary.			

What I can do to raise my grade	
I can raise my grade in Assignment 1 by …	
I can raise my grade in Assignment 2 by …	
I can raise my grade in Assignment 3 by …	
My target grade for Component 3 is:	

Objectives

In this unit you will:

- Explore what is involved in the test
- Select topics for talks
- Prepare for the Individual Talk, including cue cards
- Prepare for the Conversation

- Explore what examiners are looking for
- Practise for the Individual Talk and Conversation
- Review your progress and how to raise your grade

As well as taking Paper 1, and Paper 2 or Component 3, you may also be doing the optional Speaking and Listening Test. The Individual Talk gives you the opportunity to demonstrate how well you can prepare and organise material on a topic of your choice, communicate with an audience and use a range of language. This leads into the Conversation in which you can show how well you can discuss wider issues around your topic.

This unit will help you to understand what is involved in the test, the assessment objectives and what examiners are looking for. Work through the unit, then answer the review questions at the end to monitor your progress.

 Review

Component 4 – Speaking and Listening Test is optional

You may take this optional part of the Cambridge IGCSE First Language English exam in addition to the other components.

What is involved in the Speaking and Listening Test

In this test you give a short Individual Talk (Part 1) on a single topic of your choice, then engage in a Conversation (Part 2) with your teacher and/or an examiner. Your talk should flow naturally for about 3–4 minutes but if you get stuck or simply go blank with nerves your teacher or examiner will try to help you. The teacher or examiner may interrupt with questions and will begin Part 2 if your Individual Talk goes over 4½ minutes. The Conversation should last for 7–8 minutes, so the whole test will be 10–12 minutes long.

Your test will be recorded and you may only take it once. You can use a dictionary while preparing your talk, but it may not be taken into the test.

Assessment objectives

The Individual Talk tests your speaking skills
You need to show how well you can:

- articulate experience and express what you think, feel and imagine
- present facts, ideas and opinions in a cohesive order
- communicate clearly and purposefully using fluent language
- use an appropriate register for the test and your subject matter
- hold your listener's interest.

The Conversation tests your speaking and listening skills
You need to show how well you can:

- identify and discuss what is thought, felt and imagined
- present facts, ideas and opinions in a cohesive order and hold your listener's interest
- communicate clearly and purposefully using fluent language
- understand and use an appropriate register
- listen and respond in a conversation.

The Speaking and Listening Test is internally assessed by your teacher and externally moderated by examiners. It is worth 40 marks, but is separately endorsed and the marks are not added to your final grade. The marks are divided:

- 20 marks for speaking in the Individual Talk (Part 1)
- 10 marks for speaking and 10 marks for listening in the Conversation (Part 2).

Choosing a suitable topic

In the Individual Talk, you need to be able to talk on your chosen topic on your own for 3–4 minutes. The topic you choose should also offer possibilities for the Conversation that follows. This means it is important to choose a topic that interests you and/or that you feel strongly about.

Start by listing possible topics for your talk. You might find some of the following ideas interesting:

- sport as a spectator entertainment
- money in sport today
- history of a famous sports or chess tournament
- history of tennis
- history of pop music
- Hollywood film stars in the "Golden age" of cinema
- role of the press in creating a celebrity
- a local nature reserve
- mountaineering
- surfing
- non-governmental organisations and charity
- a little-known artist
- a famous artist and how he/she became famous
- traditional music
- folk music

- how guitars are made
- climate change
- plastics
- genetic engineering
- keeping pets in cities
- exotic pets
- history of a city block or a local town
- a local festival
- farm products and pesticides
- gun laws
- fashion and/or the clothing industry in my country
- history of a designer label
- a famous designer
- an unsung hero
- my favourite author

After listing possible topics, do some initial research to assess which one(s) might be most suitable for the Individual Talk and the Conversation. You should try to make your Individual Talk lively and interesting, so think about how you might do that. You could consider being more creative and, for example, using a different 'voice' or presenting a dramatic monologue. In addition, try to think up questions that could crop up about the wider topic in the Conversation. If you cannot think of six questions that could be asked, the topic is unlikely to be suitable.

Your teacher is allowed to advise you on deciding on the best topic, so take their advice too. Here are some words of advice on a few popular topics.

1 A famous person or somebody you admire
This is a good option if the person is more than just a celebrity. A celebrity or famous person who has struggled to reach stardom or is an active campaigner for the environment or human rights will provide interesting biographical details for you to discuss.

2 Your hobby
This is a good option if you can also explain why you do it, what you gain from it and how it contributes to your daily life or well-being. Don't fall into the trap of reciting the names of famous people who do the same hobby or famous events in the hobby unless you can explain what made them famous.

3 A recent film or television series
This is a good option if you can discuss different aspects of the production and direction, and not just talk about the actors. Find out about the directors, what the film or series is based on, and why you think producers were willing to risk a lot of money making it. You will have to explain what the film or series is about so remember it is a form of fiction and not real life, and don't fall into the trap of just retelling the story. Treat the subject more as meaningful drama than passive entertainment.

4 A dramatic monologue
You could take on the role of a character in a book or film, or become a famous person such as an explorer or scientist, and present your personal history and discoveries. If you are good at drama and/or a confident speaker, this is a good option, but you need to have extra material about your topic and/or persona (character) to discuss in the Conversation. This is also a good option if you are shy when speaking to strangers as playing the part of a character can help overcome shyness.

Part 1 – Individual Talk

When you have decided on your topic, do plenty of background reading and research to have lots of information at your fingertips. Remember, your teacher and examiner will be assessing how well you can prepare and organise material, as well as how well you present information and ideas in the Individual Talk.

Planning and preparing your talk

Although your teacher can advise you on the suitability of a topic, they cannot help you to prepare your material.

First, be clear about the message and purpose of your talk. There needs to be an element of entertaining to keep your listeners interested, but your talk also needs to inform. This will indicate the sort of conclusion that will be effective. Map out ideas for your talk, including an introduction, structured points and a memorable conclusion. Remember, your tone of voice will need to engage your listeners.

Also consider if, and how, you want to use illustrations or other visual aids to support your talk. You are allowed to use a limited number, which may include maps, diagrams, statistics and pictures. They can only be used to support the content of your talk, not as a form of visual script.

> **Exam tip**
>
> Do not be distracted if your teacher or examiner makes notes while you are talking. They are just making notes on appropriate questions to ask in the Conversation that follows.

Exam tip

- You are not allowed to take extensive notes into the test or read from, or memorise, a script.
- Remember, your teacher and examiner will be assessing how well you can select and use a range of language devices. You can use a dictionary to prepare your talk but it may not be taken into the test.

Apply

1 Choose one of the ideas for a talk on page 95 or an idea of your own that you know something about. Then do some research to gather ideas about the approach you will take and information for the content.

2 Plan ideas for your talk in the planning frame below, but remember that these are just guidelines and you must not write a script. Then consider how you will display or incorporate any visual aids.

3 Practise delivering a talk based on your ideas. You can do this on your own, recording your talk so that you can listen to it later and consider improvements. However, also practise delivering the talk to a classmate or someone at home so that you can consider their feedback.

4 Time your talk and make sure you can deliver it in 3–4 minutes.

My topic	
Introduction	
What the topic is about	
Why I chose this topic	
Why it is of interest or special features to grab attention	
Main body: at least five key points, arranged to lead to a conclusion, including language devices I could use	
1	
2	
3	
4	

5	

Conclusion: something dramatic or surprising, or a detail that will lead to discussion

Preparing a cue card

You may take one cue card of about postcard size into the exam room. You may use only one side of the card for your key points but not write continuous sentences. It must also be labelled with your name and candidate number.

A student called Katya chose the history of the spice trade as her topic. It is a good topic because it offers a great deal to talk about. It offers an opportunity for Katya to present facts and data, thoughts and personal opinions, all of which can be developed in Part 2. The teacher and examiner will be informed about something they can relate to because we all use spices in one way or another.

✏ Apply

1 Look on page 98 at the three different cue cards Katya wrote and decide which one was appropriate and helped her most.

2 Return to the topic you chose in the last activity and write an appropriate cue card in the space below.

A – History of spice

Spices were known and important during ancient times and the Middle Ages. The origins of the spice trade go back before Ancient Egyptians traded with Greece. Greek merchants traded with India and got as far as south-eastern Asia. Spices led to the creation of vast empires. The Dutch and English took spices from Asia into Europe. When Europeans started using spices like cinnamon, pepper, ginger, cloves and vanilla, they travelled to Asia to bring them home. People used spices to flavour their food and disguise when it had gone bad, but also for medicinal uses. Some were used to preserve food and make it last longer, we still do this today. We still use spice in food and for some medicines. The old trick of putting a clove next to a bad tooth still works. In the 17th century, European nations started setting up trading posts in Asia and conquered entire islands for nutmeg. Sailing ships brought expensive spices from Indonesia and parts of India because they could not grow them in colder parts of Europe.

B – History of spice

Intro: Define spice – brief history of spice – origins & primitive people

Uses: medicinal and flavouring, scents and cosmetics

Trade: ancient times and the Middle Ages: Venice – India – Asia – then New World

Empires built on trade: Dutch & English: cinnamon, pepper, cumin, cloves, vanilla

17th c trade wars – ships – Dutch & English East India Companies

European trading posts: Asia & nutmeg islands – led to colonialism

Caribbean islands & French: vanilla still a major trade – current price

If time: most popular spices today & why

C – History of spice

Intro & why I chose topic   Trade
Origins of spice trade   Colonialism
Purposes & uses   Modern uses

Part 2 – Conversation

The Conversation that follows your talk will be about your chosen topic and about 7–8 minutes long. It is designed to assess how well you can engage in conversation and how well you listen to what somebody is saying or asking.

Expect your teacher or examiner to ask open-ended questions to encourage you to say more. They may start questions with: "Tell me more about ...", "Why did ..." or "How ...?". For example, they may ask about why you chose your topic. This is where you can pick up marks on what you think, feel and imagine.

You will need to engage your teacher or examiner in a two-way conversation, giving full answers to their questions and avoiding "Yes" and "No" answers. You must be prepared to give more factual information than was in your talk and to add extra interesting details. You should also be prepared to express and defend your point of view, even if your teacher or examiner does not share it.

Preparing for the Conversation

To prepare for the Conversation, think of questions that your teacher or examiner might ask. Think of questions using the following words to imagine what you might be asked about.

If you find this difficult, practise with a friend or someone at home and ask them to think up challenging questions to test your knowledge of the wider issues in the topic. Also think of ways to express your personal views and opinions about the topic.

Here are some suggestions of how you can develop topics in the Conversation.

 **QuestionRecap**

Revisit the assessment objectives on page 93, which include discussing what you think, feel and imagine.

Exam tip

Use an appropriate register throughout the Conversation. Be polite and explain your views as objectively as possible.

---

1 A famous person or somebody you admire
An account of meeting a famous person could be developed into a discussion of wider issues such as what makes a celebrity, privacy and media intrusion. A talk about a famous sports personality could be extended into why the sport is popular and/or your opinions on why people want to know more about particular players.

2 Your hobby
A talk about your hobby could be developed into a discussion about its history and what attracted you to the hobby in the first place.

3 A recent film or television series
A talk about a film could be developed into discussion of age-ratings, censorship and/or your opinions on popular culture and the film industry.

4 A dramatic monologue
A dramatic monologue can be developed to discuss the character's personality and achievements and/or struggles more objectively. You can include how different people see this person, as well as your personal opinion.

✏️ **Apply**

Choose any of the topics you have already considered.

1 Write questions you might be asked in a conversation about this topic.

....

....

....

....

....

2 Decide what visual aids you would use for this topic, and why.

....

....

....

Transcript of a sample conversation

✏️ **Apply**

1 Read the following transcript of part of Katya's conversation with her teacher on the history of spices. Pay particular attention to what the teacher asks and how the questions are framed. Try to identify how the teacher encourages Katya to discuss what she thinks, feels and imagines. (The symbol [...] indicates parts that are not included here.)

2 Turn to the marking guide for Component 4 Part 2 on pages 207–08. Decide what marks you would give Katya for this part of the test. There are 10 marks for speaking and 10 marks for listening.

3 Compare the marks you have given Katya with the examiner's marks and comments on page 102.

Teacher (T): This is a fascinating topic. How did you become interested in it, Katya?

An open question asking for a personal response

Katya (K): From our food technology classes. My family like spicy food and I have been making different dishes at home from different parts of the world. All of them use spices and I realised I was using the same jars and packets over and over again. [...] I'm also doing History and Business Studies, and this was something we looked at last term – briefly. I've combined my personal interest with history.

Asks not for a correct answer, but for Katya to speculate and suggest her ideas or opinions

T: You say the spice trade has ancient origins. Why did people first start using spices, do you think?

K: According to what I've read, we've been using spices and herbs since people lived in caves. I've no idea how they discovered that certain spices and herbs cured bad stomachs, for example – trial and error, I suppose – but there is evidence that monks in what is now the Netherlands were using cloves and cinnamon as early as the 8th century. A famous herbalist called Culpepper wrote a big book about remedies in the 17th century. Housewives had recipes for toothache and baby colic using cloves and other spices long before that, though. [...]

T: My dentist still uses oil of cloves to help toothache.

K: That is an ancient trick to kill pain. It doesn't taste too good, though. I've tried it. [Makes a face.] Originally, pepper was used by apothecaries as a medication. It was difficult to get, though. That's why it was so expensive.

T: You say that this trade led to the development of great empires. Can you expand on that a bit more?

K: Well, the Dutch, for example, found nutmeg only grew on certain islands. The trade was very lucrative – there was a lot of money to be made – so some Dutch traders and sailors found a way – a very cruel way – to get rid of all the natives growing nutmeg on one island so they could develop it for themselves. On another island, they burned down all the trees to stop any competition. It was very cruel. The interesting thing is that one person managed to keep one single clove of nutmeg and this grew into a tree, and now there is nutmeg and mace on the island again – and they export it to Europe now, for their own benefit.

T: And was that the start of the Dutch colonisation of the East Indies? How do you feel about that?

K: Burning down the trees? It was a terrible thing to do. It destroyed whole families and changed an island's way of life forever. If you look at the long-term business side, though, I suppose it helped to make the Dutch successful traders and that helped the people living in Amsterdam.

T: So you have mixed feelings?

K: No, not really. I think what they did was cruel and wrong. But I can see how they would have argued for it at the time.

T: Well, our time is running out. One last question: you say the price of vanilla is now very expensive. This is one of many people's favourite scents and flavourings. Is there an alternative? What will happen if we can't get vanilla for our ice-cream?

K: Synthetic substitutes. They are already being used. In fact, the fragrance industry – for candles and room sprays – use chemicals all the time.

T: And that is better for the vanilla growers?

K: Hardly – well, I suppose it depends on your point of view – whether you are growing it or just selling it.

T: Thank you, Katya, that was a very interesting conversation. We could go on for much longer but we have stop here.

K: Thank you for being so interested.

Prompts Katya to say more on the topic and/or express her opinion

Katya has relaxed and her tone and register become less formal

Asks for more details, not a right or wrong answer

Asks Katya to express her opinion, which she needs to justify or support with an example

Very good: Katya shows that she understands both sides of the argument

Open question asks for a personal response

Demonstrates Katya's thinking skills although she doesn't have time to develop her views

Ends by showing there is more to discuss and that she is still in full control of her material. She has not run out of things to say

Examiner comments

Speaking: 10 marks

Student develops and extends her topic very well. She elicits responses from her listener and speaks on equal terms in a fluent, natural conversation. Some words are repeated ("cruel"), but the tone is modified to show this is deliberate. Changes of tone are also used for emphasis and for humour and irony. She speaks in full control of the material and with some eloquence. Appropriate and accurate use of language is maintained throughout.

Listening: 10 marks

A natural and fluent conversation. Student responds fully to questions and develops the prompts intelligently. Demonstrates confidence when the conversation takes a new turn. She has obvious enthusiasm for her topic throughout.

Total: 20/20 marks

Practising talks and conversations

Now you have an opportunity to plan and practise presenting a talk and having an exam-style conversation.

✎ Apply

1 Working with a partner, each choose a different topic.

2 Make a plan for your own talk and organise how you are going to present it. Use the planning frame on page 103.

3 Draft your cue card and make a note of any visual aids you want to use in the space below.

4 Discuss your plans and cue card with your partner, then make any changes necessary.

5 Take turns to present your talks to each other. Practise each talk at least twice, then assess each other using the table below.

Assessment for Part 1	Very good	Adequate	Can be improved	Needs much more practice
Speaking skills				
Knowledge of subject				
Clear beginning, middle and end				
Lively, interesting presentation				
Wide range of vocabulary				
Appropriate tone, irony and/or humour for emphasis and effect				
Does not rely on visual aids for help				

My topic	
Introduction	
What the topic is about	
Why I chose this topic	
Why it is of interest or special features to grab attention	
Main body: at least five key points, arranged to lead to a conclusion	
1	
2	
3	
4	
5	
Conclusion: something dramatic or surprising, or a detail that will lead to discussion	

✏️ **Apply**

1. Working with the same partner, practise conversations for Part 2. Take it in turns to engage each other in conversation about your topics.

2. Assess your conversation skills, using the table below.

Assessment for Part 2	Very good	Adequate	Can be improved	Needs much more practice
Speaking skills				
Extends topic in new ways				
Answers questions fluently				
Appropriate register				
Wide range of vocabulary				
Appropriate tone, irony and/or humour for emphasis and effect				
Listening skills				
Responds fully to questions				
Develops prompts in interesting ways				
Makes confident replies				
Aware of new directions in conversation				
Natural and fluent conversation techniques				

 Link

You can see how an examiner would mark your talk and conversation on pages 207–08.

Review

Think about what you have learned about Component 4. Fill out the questionnaire below from memory.

Choosing a topic	
Writing a cue card	
Selecting visual aids	
What examiners want to hear in Part 1	
What to expect in Part 2	
The sort of questions asked in Part 2	
How I can show I am a good listener in Part 2	
Other thoughts and comments on preparing and practising for this test	

Raise your grade

Fill out the questionnaire below to assess your progress, then make notes on what you can do to raise your grade.

	Struggling	Improve	Good
Reading skills (Parts 1 and 2)			
I can explain facts and data.			
I can discuss my thoughts and feelings.			
I can communicate clearly.			
I can develop ideas and opinions in conversation.			
I can use different registers.			
I can modify or change my tone for effect.			
Listening skills (Part 2)			
I can identify a speaker's register.			
I can identify change in a speaker's tone.			
I can identify facts and understand data.			
I can understand a speaker's thoughts and opinions.			
I can understand a wide range of vocabulary.			

What I can do to raise my grade	
I can raise my grade in Part 1 by …	
I can raise by grade in Part 2 by …	
My target grade for Component 4 is:	

Objectives

In this unit you will:

- Review your reading skills
- Improve your word and sentence skills
- Practise writing better summaries
- Identify ways to understand the writer's craft better
- Review your progress and how to raise your grade

Good language skills will help you do your best in all parts of your exams. This unit focuses on how you will need to use them in Paper 1.

Paper 1 tests your reading skills in different ways. You need to show how well you:

- understand explicit meanings, facts and data
- understand implicit meanings (what is being said between the lines)
- understand how writers choose their words for a particular effect.

⏪ QuestionRecap

In Paper 1 there will be 3 texts: A, B, C.

- Make sure you read the texts thoroughly first. Skim and scan later.
- Skimming is quickly casting an eye over text to recap what it is about. You will use this when you *re-read* a text before answering a specific question.
- Scanning is reading text to locate specific information. You will need this skill in the vocabulary questions to find a word or phrase.

Reading more efficiently

As you go through school, you acquire the habit of reading with different levels of concentration, perhaps without even realising it. Now you are preparing for your exams, you need to make sure you are reading as efficiently as possible. Practise some of the reading and language skills you need for Paper 1.

Skimming and scanning

Two important reading skills you need to develop are skimming and scanning, especially for answering questions in Paper 1 Question 1.

✏️ Apply

Practise your skimming and scanning techniques by locating information in the following sample Paper 1 Question 1.

1 Read Text A, "A cheese with a sting – the story of the Picodon of Provence" very closely, then read sample Question 1(a)–(e).

2 Skim Text A to remind yourself what it is about and where different sub-topics are located. You might look particularly at the headings and beginnings of paragraphs.

3 Re-read each question, scanning the text for the particular information, words and/or phrases you are asked to find and/or comment on. You might find it useful to run a finger under the text as you scan. Use a pencil or coloured pencil(s) to write the question number and letter in the margin of the text when you identify or locate relevant details.

4 Compare your annotations with how another student annotated the text, on page 111.

> **Exam tip**
>
> Avoid using highlighters because you cannot get rid of the marks if you make a mistake.

 Answers can be found online at **www.oxfordsecondary.com/esg-for-caie-igcse**

Text A: A cheese with a sting – the story of the Picodon of Provence

This text is about a special type of cheese produced in France. (It is slightly longer than you will get in an exam to give you more practice.)

The Picodon is not a cheese, it is a flattened round of history, a taste of home for anyone living in la Drôme or l'Ardèche region of Provence in France. But no two Picodons are alike. Poor quality Picodons taste soapy, metallic or even of potatoes; good picodons taste of goat "caprine",
5   and sting.

The first written reference to the cheese was in 1361, in Dieulefit, which to this day has its own specific stamp for the Prince of Picodons, made by the Dieulefit method. In 1367, two unlucky merchants taking their Picodons by donkey-cart to market in Montélimar were attacked and their
10   cheeses stolen. Even the name "Picodon" shows its fine pedigree; there is general agreement that it derives from the local patois "picau", meaning "piquant" or stinging the tongue. A good Picodon will do just that and the older the Picodon the stronger its sting.

So strong is Picodon nostalgia, that there are letters home from the front in
15   the First World War, thanking mothers and wives for the cheeses they sent. One such notes that the Picodons were "so good that there is only one left" and the soldier was "content that Marie is looking after the goats so well and is so sensible and my little Jean too, but I mustn't think of them too much or I will feel terrible." In his day, it would have been his
20   wife, his mother, or his grandmother who actually made the Picodon. Goats were "the cows of the poor" and it was the women who made the goat cheese, handing the recipes down through the family in a purely oral tradition.

It was not only the peasants who missed their Picodons; in the 1890s, when
25   the Montélimar politician M. Emile Loubet became President of France, he organised a weekly consignment of his favourite cheese to be sent to him in Paris. He must have missed the arrival of the local market day train, nicknamed "le Picodon", which made seventeen stops on its route […] from Dieulefit to Montélimar market, twenty-eight kilometres away.

30   The Picodon also lays claim to being the only cheese to have gone into space, sneaked onto the 1996 NASA Columbia space mission by a Drômoise astronaut and medical specialist. Jean-Jacques Favier defied the US ground laws regarding unpasteurised cheeses to take seventeen Picodons, one for each day of orbit, as part of his personal allowance. Having had Picodons
35   confiscated in the past, the only way he could get them past American customs officials was by mailing them to his address in the USA. So popular were the cheeses with the crew of seven, that the astronauts held their reunion at the Picodon Fête at Saou, a traditional annual celebration.

From *A Small Cheese in Provence* by Jean Gill

📖 **Activity**

Sample Question 1

(a) Give **two** qualities of a good Picodon cheese according to the text.

- ....

- ....

[2]

(b) Using your own words, explain what the text means by:

   (i) "So strong is Picodon nostalgia" (line 14) ....

   ....

[2]

   (ii) "In his day" (line 19) ....

   ....

[2]

(c) Re-read paragraph 2 ("The first written reference … its 'sting'.")
Give **two** reasons we know Picodon cheese has a long history.

- ....

- ....

[2]

(d) Re-read paragraphs 3, 4 and 5 ("So strong is Picodon nostalgia … annual celebration.")

   (i) Identify **two** people who were able to enjoy their Picodon cheeses far from home.

   ....

   ....

[2]

   (ii) Explain how the recipe for Picodon cheese-making has been passed down through history and by whom.

   ....

   ....

[2]

(e) Re-read paragraph 5 ("The Picodon also … annual celebration.")
Using your own words, explain how a small cheese from Provence
went into space.

....

....

....

[3]

Look at how a student has skimmed and scanned the text to locate her answers and compare your skills.

Text A: A cheese with a sting – the story of the Picodon of Provence

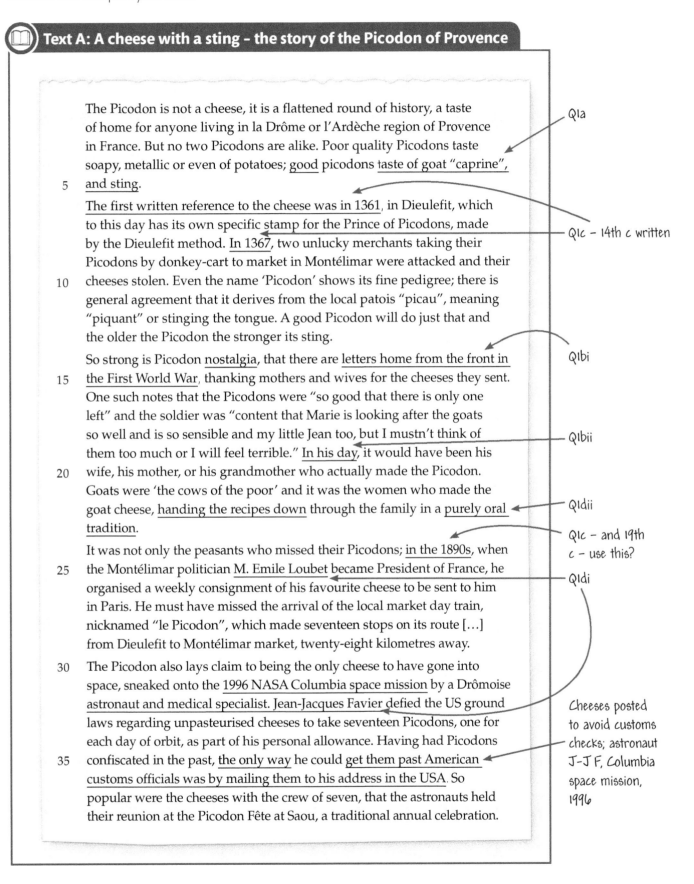

The Picodon is not a cheese, it is a flattened round of history, a taste of home for anyone living in la Drôme or l'Ardèche region of Provence in France. But no two Picodons are alike. Poor quality Picodons taste soapy, metallic or even of potatoes; good picodons taste of goat "caprine",
5 and sting.

    Q1a

The first written reference to the cheese was in 1361, in Dieulefit, which to this day has its own specific stamp for the Prince of Picodons, made by the Dieulefit method. In 1367, two unlucky merchants taking their Picodons by donkey-cart to market in Montélimar were attacked and their
10 cheeses stolen. Even the name 'Picodon' shows its fine pedigree; there is general agreement that it derives from the local patois "picau", meaning "piquant" or stinging the tongue. A good Picodon will do just that and the older the Picodon the stronger its sting.

    Q1c – 14th c written

So strong is Picodon nostalgia, that there are letters home from the front in
15 the First World War, thanking mothers and wives for the cheeses they sent. One such notes that the Picodons were "so good that there is only one left" and the soldier was "content that Marie is looking after the goats so well and is so sensible and my little Jean too, but I mustn't think of them too much or I will feel terrible." In his day, it would have been his
20 wife, his mother, or his grandmother who actually made the Picodon. Goats were 'the cows of the poor' and it was the women who made the goat cheese, handing the recipes down through the family in a purely oral tradition.

    Q1bi

    Q1bii

    Q1dii

It was not only the peasants who missed their Picodons; in the 1890s, when
25 the Montélimar politician M. Emile Loubet became President of France, he organised a weekly consignment of his favourite cheese to be sent to him in Paris. He must have missed the arrival of the local market day train, nicknamed "le Picodon", which made seventeen stops on its route […] from Dieulefit to Montélimar market, twenty-eight kilometres away.

    Q1c – and 19th c – use this?

    Q1di

30 The Picodon also lays claim to being the only cheese to have gone into space, sneaked onto the 1996 NASA Columbia space mission by a Drômoise astronaut and medical specialist. Jean-Jacques Favier defied the US ground laws regarding unpasteurised cheeses to take seventeen Picodons, one for each day of orbit, as part of his personal allowance. Having had Picodons
35 confiscated in the past, the only way he could get them past American customs officials was by mailing them to his address in the USA. So popular were the cheeses with the crew of seven, that the astronauts held their reunion at the Picodon Fête at Saou, a traditional annual celebration.

Cheeses posted to avoid customs checks; astronaut J-J F, Columbia space mission, 1996

Improving language skills at word and sentence level

Word level

Most of us know more words than we use in everyday conversation; we have a wider passive vocabulary than active. Test yourself to see how many words you use on an everyday basis, how many similar ones you actually know and how many others you can find.

Apply

1 From memory, what will examiners be looking for in your vocabulary in Paper 1?

Vocabulary: ....

Check your answer in the marking guidelines for Paper 1 on pages 201–02.

2 Read the words in the table below.

  a Without using a thesaurus, write as many words as you can with the same or similar meaning in the second column.

  b Now use a thesaurus to add any other words in the third column.

Word	Words of same or similar meaning (without thesaurus)	Words of same or similar meaning (with thesaurus)
Look		
Start		
Stop		
Speak		
Run		
Walk		

Exam tip

When writing your compositions, check that you have used a variety of sentence structures and whether any can be improved.

Sentence level

Writers use sentences of different lengths and structures to vary pace and create specific effects, such as tension or drama, in their writing. You will be asked to discuss these techniques in Paper 1 Question 2. Using different sentence structures yourself will help to improve your marks for all the writing tasks in the exams.

✎ Apply

1 From memory, what are examiners looking for in your sentences in Paper 1?

Sentences: ....

2 Write down what you remember about each type of sentence in this table.

Simple	
Minor	
Compound	
Complex	
Interrogative	
Imperative	

3 Punctuate the following paragraph, then count how many different types of sentence you have created. (You will find a suggested answer on page 133.)

Aromatherapy is a type of herbal healing the word is coined from two words aroma which means pleasant scent and therapy which means treatment the scents used are not perfumes but the pure essential oils of plants that are valued for their therapeutic properties some of the plants used in aromatherapy are quite common and easy to grow such as lavender and rose others are rarer and are more expensive to obtain frankincense is one of the most expensive it is valued for its fragrant calming properties.

Word and sentence level

✎ Apply

1 Practise using wider vocabulary and varying sentence structures by rewriting the paragraph below to create a gripping opening or ending for a narrative composition in Paper 2 or Component 3. Change words and vary the sentences for a more exciting effect. Remember to start a new line for each new person speaking.

Jo and Pepe ran and ran. They got very tired, but they kept on running. When they stopped, they were too tired to speak. Eventually, Jo said, "I think we can stop running now." "No," said Pepe, looking over Jo's shoulder. "Look what's coming." Jo looked then started running again without waiting for Pepe.

....

....

....

....

....

....

....

⏪ Recap

- Connectives are very useful for linking clauses to make complex sentences. They include: conjunctions (e.g. so, and, until); adverbs (e.g. then, finally, therefore); phrases (e.g. as a result, on the other hand).
- When trying to write with more impact, comparatives and superlatives can be very useful, as long as you use them correctly.

Link

In the *Complete First Language English for Cambridge IGCSE® Student Book*, you can find information on the rules for writing dialogue on page 215 and rules for comparison and superlatives on pages 284–85.

2 Correct these sentences so the meaning stays the same. You may need to change the wording.

   a Playing football is more easy than playing rugby.

   ....

   b Arlo's composition was a more perfect story than mine.

   ....

   c Clara's artwork is the most unique in our class, nobody can do what she does.

   ....

   ....

   d Kelvin and Angela usually get top marks in mathematics but Angela is modester than Kelvin, who boasts a lot; he's much more boasting than her.

   ....

   ....

   ....

3 To avoid repetition and demonstrate your vocabulary, rephrase these sentences. You may have to rewrite the sentence. Look out for redundant words.

   a I'm not unhappy, but I was happier when we were on holiday, much more happier than I am now.

   ....

   ....

   b Tom often felt lonely at weekends, but he felt more lonely during the summer vacation.

   ....

   ....

   c Grandparents are supposed to be more kinder than parents, but their grandparents weren't kind, they were more stricter and meaner than even the most cruellest parents in fictitious made up stories.

   ....

   ....

   ....

QuestionRecap

Remember that you must use your own words in your summary. This means you must not use the words from the text, unless you quote a word or short phrase in quotation marks.

Writing a better summary

You will write a much better summary for Paper 1 Question 1(f) if you identify exactly the appropriate information in the text, then organise the information in the best way to include it in the summary. You can also use punctuation to help you write as concisely as possible.

Identifying and organising information

 Apply

1. Read Text B, "The seven ages of appetite" very thoroughly, then read sample Question 1(f).
2. Skim and/or scan the text to find the information you need to answer the question. Use two different coloured pencils to locate information for the two parts of the question. You must use your own words in your summary so prepare for that by annotating the text in your own words.
3. Use numbers and letters to help you organise the information in preparation for writing your summary.
4. Then look at how a successful student annotated his text on pages 117–18.

Exam tip

Annotate and organise information in the text, *before* you start writing.

 QuestionRecap

There are 10 marks available for the content of your summary, so you must find at least ten points to write about.

Text B: The seven ages of appetite

This text is about how a person's appetite can develop and change through a lifetime. (The text is slightly longer than you will get in an exam to give you more practice.)

Everyone's relationship with food differs depending on cost, availability, family preferences, even peer pressure. But what we all share is appetite: our desire to eat. Babies instinctively know when they need feeding. As we get
5   older, however, our desire for food has both a physical and psychological dimension. Our appetite is not fixed, it changes across our lifespan as we age. As our choice of food is an important factor in our health and well-being throughout our lives, it's important that we get into the
10   right habits when young. As Shakespeare might have put it, there are seven ages of appetite.

In early childhood the body goes through rapid growth. Children are always hungry for this reason, but their eating habits need to be monitored. Being greedy as a
15   child can lead to being overweight as an adult. Being an over-fussy eater can have the opposite effect. Parents need to create tasting strategies to help small children learn about unfamiliar but important foods such as green vegetables. On the other hand, being forced to "clear the
20   plate" by parents can lead to overeating in later years. There are currently growing calls for governments to protect children from targeted junk food advertising, which increases unnecessary food consumption.

During adolescence, teenagers experience a growth in
25   appetite and stature driven by hormones signalling

the arrival of puberty and the development from child into adult. How a teenager approaches food during this critical period will shape their lifestyle choices in later years. As young adults, lifestyle changes such as going to

30   college, marriage and parenthood all affect eating habits. It is vital to have a balanced diet at this time to stay fit and healthy and prepare for middle age, when fat is difficult to shed. Different foods send different signals to the brain. It's far too easy to consume an entire tub of ice

35   cream, for example, because fat doesn't trigger signals in the brain for us to stop eating. Foods high in protein, water or fibre content make us feel fuller for longer.

Adult working life brings other challenges, including the effects of stress, which can result in poor

40   eating habits: some people gorge; some lose their appetite. Personality traits can also play a part here: perfectionism and over-conscientiousness can affect stress and eating behaviour.

After the age of 50, the body loses muscle mass and

45   begins a steady course into old age. This is called *sarcopenia* and less physical activity can accelerate the decline. A healthy, varied diet and physical activity are essential factors in reducing the unhealthy effects of ageing. A major challenge today in the face of

50   increasing life expectancy is to maintain quality of life for the elderly, or we will become a society of very old, infirm or disabled people.

Based on "How a better understanding of the seven ages of appetite could help us stay healthy" by Alex Johnstone

 **Activity**

Sample Question 1

(f) According to **Text B**, what are the seven ages of appetite and how will understanding them help us to stay healthy?

You must **use continuous writing** (not note form) and **use your own words** as far as possible.

Your summary should be no more than 120 words.

Up to 10 marks are available for the content of your answer and up to 5 marks for the quality of your writing.

[15]

Text B: The seven ages of appetite

Everyone's relationship with food differs depending on cost, availability, family preferences, even peer pressure. But what we all share is appetite: our desire to eat. Babies instinctively know when they need feeding. As we get
5   older, however, our desire for food has both a physical and psychological dimension. Our appetite is not fixed, it changes across our lifespan as we age. As our choice of food is an important factor in our health and well-being throughout our lives, it's important that we get into the
10 right habits when young. As Shakespeare might have put it, there are seven ages of appetite.

In early childhood the body goes through rapid growth. Children are always hungry for this reason, but their eating habits need to be monitored. Being greedy as a
15 child can lead to being overweight as an adult. Being an over-fussy eater can have the opposite effect. Parents need to create tasting strategies to help small children learn about unfamiliar but important foods such as green vegetables. On the other hand, being forced to "clear the
20 plate" by parents can lead to overeating in later years. There are currently growing calls for governments to protect children from targeted junk food advertising, which increases unnecessary food consumption.

During adolescence, teenagers experience a growth in
25 appetite and stature driven by hormones signalling the arrival of puberty and the development from child into adult. How a teenager approaches food during this critical period will shape their lifestyle choices in later years. As young adults, lifestyle changes such as going to
30 college, marriage and parenthood all affect eating habits. It is vital to have a balanced diet at this time to stay fit and healthy and prepare for middle age, when fat is difficult to shed. Different foods send different signals to the brain. It's far too easy to consume an entire tub of ice
35 cream, for example, because fat doesn't trigger signals in the brain for us to stop eating. Foods high in protein, water or fibre content make us feel fuller for longer.

Adult working life brings other challenges, including the effects of stress, which can result in poor
40 eating habits: some people gorge; some lose their appetite. Personality traits can also play a part here: perfectionism and over-conscientiousness can affect stress and eating behaviour.

After the age of 50, the body loses muscle mass and
45 begins a steady course into old age. This is called *sarcopenia* and less physical activity can accelerate the

---

Margin annotations:

Instinct tells them they need food/ Babies only eat what's necessary

1 – first age

2 – second age

Must learn to eat in healthy manner

Children need plenty of good food, but not too much (so not overweight) or too little

3

Teenagers need to understand healthy eating habits so they can have healthy life-styles as adults

4

5

Young adults need to understand how diet will affect them in middle age and avoid eating disorders from stress

6

Unhealthy diet leads to ill-health later so avoid bad diets/ habits

decline. A healthy, <u>varied diet and physical activity</u>
<u>are essential factors in reducing the unhealthy effects</u>
<u>of ageing.</u> A major challenge today in the face of
50 increasing life expectancy is to <u>maintain quality of life</u>
<u>for the elderly,</u> or we will become a society of very old,
infirm or disabled people.

7

Understanding
how a varied
diet can improve
and contribute
to better quality
of life in old
age – to prevent
becoming ill or
disabled.

Vital for healthy
old-age

Link

You will find more guidance
on using colons and
semi-colons on pages 305–08
of the *Complete First Language
English for Cambridge IGCSE®
Student Book*.

Using punctuation to write concisely

Using colons and semi-colons in complex sentences can help you to write more concisely and elegantly than if you write numerous simple and compound sentences.

Apply

1 Read Text C, "Aromatherapy" below, then read sample Question 1(f) that follows.

2 Annotate the text and organise your points to prepare for answering the question.

3 Compare your notes with how another student selected details, on page 121.

4 When you have decided on the ten key points for this summary, write your answer to the question, using clear sentences in continuous writing. Try to use colons and/or semi-colons to keep your summary concise.

Text C: Aromatherapy

Aromatherapy uses natural "essential oils" extracted
from flowers and their stems, tree bark, leaves and
roots. These oils can be used to improve and enhance
our well-being, mood or general health. Inhaling
5   the aroma from essential oils is believed to stimulate
brain function. Essential oils can also be absorbed
through the skin, where they travel through to the
bloodstream and, it is believed, promote healing. This
makes aromatherapy a form of alternative medicine
10   or therapy: a therapy that is gaining momentum.
Currently, aromatherapy is used for a variety of
reasons, including pain relief, mood enhancement and
increased cognitive function.

A wide number of essential oils, each with its own
15 healing properties, are used by aromatherapists. These
oils originate in the fragrant essence of a plant. But
essential oils should not be confused with perfumes or
other fragrance oils used in cosmetics. Essential oils are
natural to the plant, whereas some fragrance oils can
20 be chemically produced to imitate aromatic scents, then
used for perfumes, colognes, candles, etc.

Essential oils are extracted in one of two ways: either by
steam distillation or by pressing. Distillation is the most
prominent method. This technique involves steaming
25 the plant matter until it breaks down into a soggy mess.
The subsequent mush becomes the plant's fragrant oil
by being cooled, then separated from any water content
and finally filtered into its pure essential oil. Some
aromatherapy oils are too concentrated at this stage to
30 apply directly to the skin and need to be combined with
a gentle carrier oil or lotion to dilute their strength.

Almond oil is a popular "carrier". Unlike applying
bottled perfumes, applying some stringent fragrant oils
to the skin can result in painful, harmful reactions such
35 as rashes or burns.

There are various types of common essential oils, including
lavender, tea tree, patchouli, jasmine, and rosemary.
Each scent has special and specific properties, which an
experienced aromatherapist can explain and advise upon.

Activity

Sample Question 1

(f) According to **Text C**, what is the difference between the scents used in aromatherapy and those
in perfumes, candles and cosmetics?

You must **use continuous writing** (not note form) and **use your own words** as far as possible.

Your summary should be no more than 120 words.

**Up to 10 marks are available for the content of your answer and up to 5 marks for
the quality of your writing.**

....

....

....

[15]

(If you need more lines, use an extra sheet of paper. Remember to write your name and the question number at the top.)

📖 **Text C: Aromatherapy**

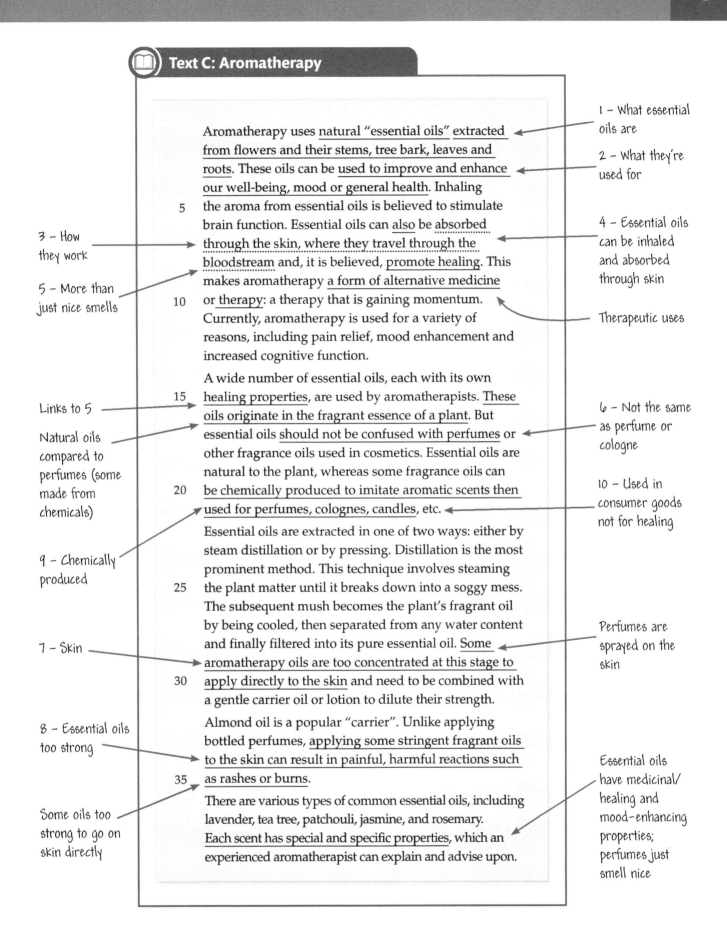

1 – What essential oils are

2 – What they're used for

4 – Essential oils can be inhaled and absorbed through skin

Therapeutic uses

3 – How they work

5 – More than just nice smells

Aromatherapy uses natural "essential oils" extracted from flowers and their stems, tree bark, leaves and roots. These oils can be used to improve and enhance our well-being, mood or general health. Inhaling
5   the aroma from essential oils is believed to stimulate brain function. Essential oils can also be absorbed through the skin, where they travel through the bloodstream and, it is believed, promote healing. This makes aromatherapy a form of alternative medicine
10   or therapy: a therapy that is gaining momentum. Currently, aromatherapy is used for a variety of reasons, including pain relief, mood enhancement and increased cognitive function.

Links to 5

Natural oils compared to perfumes (some made from chemicals)

9 – Chemically produced

A wide number of essential oils, each with its own
15   healing properties, are used by aromatherapists. These oils originate in the fragrant essence of a plant. But essential oils should not be confused with perfumes or other fragrance oils used in cosmetics. Essential oils are natural to the plant, whereas some fragrance oils can
20   be chemically produced to imitate aromatic scents then used for perfumes, colognes, candles, etc.

6 – Not the same as perfume or cologne

10 – Used in consumer goods not for healing

7 – Skin

8 – Essential oils too strong

Essential oils are extracted in one of two ways: either by steam distillation or by pressing. Distillation is the most prominent method. This technique involves steaming
25   the plant matter until it breaks down into a soggy mess. The subsequent mush becomes the plant's fragrant oil by being cooled, then separated from any water content and finally filtered into its pure essential oil. Some aromatherapy oils are too concentrated at this stage to
30   apply directly to the skin and need to be combined with a gentle carrier oil or lotion to dilute their strength.

Perfumes are sprayed on the skin

Some oils too strong to go on skin directly

Almond oil is a popular "carrier". Unlike applying bottled perfumes, applying some stringent fragrant oils to the skin can result in painful, harmful reactions such
35   as rashes or burns.

There are various types of common essential oils, including lavender, tea tree, patchouli, jasmine, and rosemary. Each scent has special and specific properties, which an experienced aromatherapist can explain and advise upon.

Essential oils have medicinal/ healing and mood-enhancing properties; perfumes just smell nice

---

✏ Apply

Read the student's summary below. Decide whether it could be improved and, if so, how.

a Make notes on what the student has done well.

....

....

....

....

....

b Make notes on the weaker areas and how the summary could be improved.

....

....

....

....

....

....

The differences between essential oils and fragrances for perfumes relate to the origins of the scents and their uses. Essential oils are obtained from plants and trees via distillation or pressing. The oils extracted are entirely natural, but not all of them can be applied directly to the skin; some need to be diluted with another oil or lotion because when ~~some essential oils~~ they are massaged into the skin they are ~~then~~ absorbed into the blood stream. Other ~~essential~~ therapeutic oils can be inhaled to stimulate or calm the mind. Scents used in perfumes and ~~scented~~ products such as candles ~~and colognes~~ can be created out of chemicals and sprayed onto the skin, or used simply because they smell pleasant, not because they have a healing effect. (119 words)

Understanding the writer's craft better

The best way to prepare for any question in the First Language English exams is to read widely. How much you read and what you read will be evident when you tackle Questions 2 and 3 in Paper 1 (and also in Paper 2). Your wide reading experience will help you to:

- understand the writer's implicit meaning (infer what is between the lines)
- discuss a writer's choice of words, including how linguistic devices and imagery have been used for particular effects
- use these skills in your own writing.

Understanding vocabulary from the context

In Paper 1, Question 2(a) you will be asked to identify a word or phrase in a text that suggests the same as certain words in the question. In Question 2(b) you will be asked to use your own words to explain what certain words in the text mean.

The best way to answer these questions is to look carefully at the context of the relevant paragraph.

Apply

1 Carefully read Text D, "Winter in Alaska" twice, then complete the notes below prompted by "wh-" questions.

- (Where) The setting is ....
- (When) The time of year is ....
- (Who) The main character is ....
- (What) Mabel goes ....
- (Why) To ....

2 Then answer the questions that follow.

Text D: Winter in Alaska

Mabel has left a comfortable life in Pennsylvania and moved to live on a farm in Alaska.

The leaden sky seemed to hold its breath. December grew near, and still there was no snow in the valley. For several days, the thermometers held at twenty-five below zero. When Mabel went out to feed the chickens, she was stunned by the cold. It cut through her skin and ached on her
5   hip bones and knuckles. She watched a few dry snowflakes fall, but it was only a dusting, and the river wind swept it against exposed rocks and stumps in small dirty drifts. It was difficult to discern the scant snow from the fine glacial silt, blown in gusts from the riverbed, that coated everything.

From *The Snow Child* by Eowyn Ivey

📖 **Activity**

Sample Question 2

(a) Identify a word or phrase from the text which suggests the same idea as the words underlined:

(i)   Mabel was <u>shocked by how cold it was.</u>

....

(ii)   There was only <u>a lightweight coating</u> of snow.

....

(b) Using your own words, explain what the writer means by each of the phrases underlined:

(i)   The <u>leaden sky</u> seemed to hold its breath.

....

(ii)   <u>It was difficult to discern</u> the scant snow from the fine glacial silt.

....

Understanding implicit meaning

✏️ **Apply**

1   Read Text E, "A Chinese take-away" on page 125. What is it about? Tick as many boxes as you think appropriate.

• Kitchen equipment	☐	• A girl who doesn't like cooking	☐
• A Chinese take-away	☐	• A girl who is afraid of her parents	☐
• Friday night in a town	☐	• A girl who wants to run away	☐
• Iron and steel	☐	• A girl with stomach problems	☐
• Different types of knives	☐	• A girl who has to make a big decision	☐

2   Re-read Text E, then answer sample Question 2(a) and (b), which follow.

Text E: A Chinese take-away

She had come to tell them of her decision.

Standing by the door of the kitchen in the semi-darkness, a faint odour of bleach and onions greeted her like an old and comfortable companion. Silence, condensed by the hum of the refrigerators, echoed through and drew her in.

5 The florescent strips flickered before exploding off the hard, sharp surfaces, pricking out the edges, threatening the shadows. This was a kitchen that spoke not of home and its comforts but of forges, armoury and battle. For now, the steel rested. The oil in the deep fryer was cool, brown and thick as treacle. The heavy iron range* stood dominating the room like an altar; the four holes cut side by side into its black metal looked curiously vulnerable to her,
10 and she resisted the temptation to cover them up with the woks that huddled upside down like turtles beneath the range.

She walked across the room to the chopping board that stood on its own. Knives and choppers of different shapes and sizes hung from one of its edges, resembling a set of monstrous teeth. She could almost hear the thud of a heavy blade cleaving through flesh and
15 bone onto the wood below. Delicately, she traced the scars on the surface. Tiny fragments of wood tickled her fingertips. In two hours her mother would come down the stairs and enter this arena. The fires would be lit, the oil would begin to bubble and steam and the steel would start to clash. She remembered Friday nights when she was a child. Friday was the busiest night of the week. People invaded the take-away in hordes after the pubs had
20 closed [and] demanded to be fed. Inside the kitchen she would sit, unable to help: the still centre in the madly spinning wheel of movement around her. She would look backwards and forwards between her father and her mother. Their faces frightened her, she could not recognise them. They were not their daytime selves, they became something impersonal, mechanical, and even monstrous. They were like the knives, slashing, paring, chopping,
25 slicing, dividing. Moving through the thick greasy white smoke like the warriors of old, advancing in the mists of dawn; they looked invincible. Every ounce of being was consumed in the task of making food. It could not be called "cooking". Cooking sounded too homely. No, like alchemists, they brought forth food out of steel and fire. Their creations subdued and sated the hungry hordes that bayed impatiently outside.

30 She walked over and bent down to pick up one of the steel woks beneath the range. She tested it for its weight, savouring the way it felt to grip the wooden handle in her hand and the tension stretching her wrist. She dropped it onto one of the holes and it made a dull clunk as it landed. She walked round and round the kitchen, circling the aluminium worktop that was the centrepiece of the room. At times, she would stride, eyes wide and blazing. Then
35 at other times her steps turned into a shuffle. She sighed and muttered, shaking her head: *I can't, I can't do it, I can't, I really can't. They can. But not me. I'm too soft: too weak, too split. I don't have it – what it takes. I will fail.*

But there was another voice in her head, saying: *you can, you can do it. Of course you can. You have had the training. You have the guts. You have stamina. That's all you need. The rest will take care
40 of itself.* She heard footsteps. She felt a shaking in the depths of her stomach. They would ask her and she would not know what to say [but] she could not stay and work in the kitchen.

From *Snowdrop* by Mei Chi Chen

*****iron range** cooking oven and hobs

📖 **Activity**

Read **Text E, *A Chinese take-away,*** and then answer **Question 2(a)–(b).**

Sample Question 2

(a) Identify a word or phrase from the text that suggests the same idea as the words underlined:

(i) She could imagine the sound of a heavy blade <u>cutting</u> through meat.

....

[1]

(ii) At times she would <u>walk purposefully</u> around the kitchen.

....

[1]

(iii) On Fridays, <u>crowds of people pushed their way into</u> the take-away.

....

[1]

(iv) The food <u>calmed the people and satisfied their hunger</u>.

....

[1]

(b) Using your own words, explain what the writer means by each of the words underlined:

[Her parents] were not their daytime selves, they became something impersonal, <u>mechanical</u>, and even monstrous. They were like the knives, slashing, paring, chopping, slicing, dividing. Moving through the thick greasy white smoke like the warriors of old, advancing in the mists of dawn; they looked <u>invincible</u>. Every ounce of being was <u>consumed</u> in the task of making food.

(i) mechanical ....

[1]

(ii) invincible ....

[1]

(iii) consumed ....

[1]

Understanding how writers create effect

In Paper 1 Question 2(c) you will be asked to choose one example from a paragraph and explain how the writer uses a word or phrase to create a specific effect, for example, to describe a situation, an experience or a feeling.

 QuestionRecap

A good way to prepare for Question 2(c) and (d) (and improve your writing skills) is to review the Glossary at www.oxfordsecondary.com/esg-for-caie-igcse. Ask a friend to test you on useful terms such as: imagery, simile, metaphor, figurative language, emotive language, symbolism, theme, connotation.

 Apply

1 Answer the Question 2(c) below about the text "Winter in Alaska" (page 123).
2 Then study three students' answers to this question and the examiner comments below.

 Activity

Sample Question 2

(c) Use **one** example from the text below to explain how the writer suggests Mabel's experience of winter in Alaska.

Use your own words in your explanation.

The leaden sky seemed to hold its breath. December grew near, and still there was no snow in the valley. For several days, the thermometers held at twenty-five below zero. When Mabel went out to feed the chickens, she was stunned by the cold.

....

....

....

....

....

....

 Examiner comments

Student A: 3/3 marks

A perceptive response to the mood and tone of the paragraph.

 Examiner comments

Student B: 2/3 marks

Student has identified an apt metaphor and given a basic explanation of its usage.

 Examiner comments

Student C: 1/3 marks

Student has not understood the question fully. Second example discounted.

Student A

The writer uses the word "leaden" to describe the sky on a winter's day. The word suggests the sky is grey and heavy like lead. It is heavy with unfallen snow. The writer is using the sky as a metaphor for what is to come; it's going to be a hard (like lead) winter and Mabel is going to suffer.

Student B

The writer uses a common phrase "hold its breath". To hold your breath is when you are frightened something might happen or will happen or you are very excited about something. It's like the sky is expecting something to happen and Mabel is too. Mabel is waiting for the snow and "holding her breath" for what's to come.

Student C

The writer tells us the thermometer has been on 25 below zero, then says the woman "was stunned by the cold" like she was surprised by it. But she lives in Alaska and it gets very cold there all the time in winter. There's only a bit of snow though.

 **QuestionRecap**

Another way to prepare for Question 2(c) and (d) (and improve your writing skills) would be to revisit some of the Writer's craft boxes in the *Complete First Language English for Cambridge IGCSE® Student Book.*

 Apply

Re-read Text E, "A Chinese take-away" on page 125, then answer Question 2(c) and (d) below.

Activity

Question 2

(c) Use **one** example of a word or phrase from the text below to explain how the writer feels in the Chinese take-away kitchen that day.

Use your own words in your explanation.

She walked over and bent down to pick up one of the steel woks beneath the range. She tested it for its weight, savouring the way it felt to grip the wooden handle in her hand and the tension stretching her wrist. She dropped it onto one of the holes and it made a dull clunk as it landed. She walked round and round the kitchen, circling the aluminium worktop that was the centrepiece of the room. At times, she would stride, eyes wide and blazing. Then at other times her steps turned into a shuffle. She sighed and muttered, shaking her head: *I can't, I can't do it, I can't, I really can 't. They can. But not me. I'm too soft: too weak, too split. I don't have it – what it takes. I will fail.*

....

....

....

[3]

(d) Re-read paragraphs 3 and 4.

- Paragraph 3 begins "The florescent strips flickered ..." and is about the kitchen in the Chinese take-away.
- Paragraph 4 begins "She walked across the room ..." and is about how her parents worked in the kitchen.

Explain how the writer uses language to convey meaning and to create effect in these paragraphs. Choose **three** examples of words or phrases from **each** paragraph to support your answer. Your choices should include the use of imagery.

Write about 200–300 words.

Up to 15 marks are available for the content of your answer.

....

....

....

....

....

....

....

[15]

(if you need more lines, use an extra sheet of paper.)

Apply

1 Read and keyword a sample Question 3 below.
2 Re-read and annotate Text E, "A Chinese take-away" on page 125 to prepare to answer the question.

Exam tip

Look for clues in the question. "Dearest Daughter" tells you that either the girl's parents were not angry with her or, if they were, she is forgiven.

 QuestionRecap

There are 15 marks for the content of your answer so spend time identifying relevant material to address the bullet points only. Think carefully about what each piece of information means, including what might be inferred. Annotate the text in your own words as the basis for your points.

 Activity

Re-read **Text E, *A Chinese take-away,*** and then answer **sample Question 3**.

Sample Question 3

You are the writer's mother or father. After your daughter leaves home, you write a letter to her, telling her that you understand her reasons for not wanting to join the family business. Include the following three memories only:

• What she used to do when she was a child and you were busy in the kitchen.
• What it used to be like on Friday nights.
• Her reasons for not wanting to join you in the business.

Write the words of your letter.

Base your letter on what you have read in **Text E**, but be careful to use your own words. Address each of the three bullet points.

Start your letter, "Dearest Daughter …".

Write about 250–350 words.

Up to 15 marks are available for the content of your answer and up to 10 marks for the quality of your writing.

....
....
....
....
....
....
....
....
....

[25]

(If you need more lines, use an extra sheet of paper. Remember to write your name and the question number at the top.)

Apply

1 Compare your keywording of a sample Question 3 with another student's below.
2 Look at how the same student has annotated Text E below. Then answer these questions in the space below.
   • What does this student think is relevant to the question?
   • What will the girl's parent be talking about in his or her letter?
   • Think about your own annotations. Do you agree with this student or has he overlooked anything?

....

....

....

....

....

....

Activity

Sample Question 3

You are the writer's mother or father. After your daughter leaves home, you write a letter to her telling her that you understand her reasons for not wanting to join the family business. Include the following three memories only:

• What she used to do when she was a child and you were you were busy in the kitchen.
• What it used to be like on Friday nights.
• Her reasons for not wanting to join you in the business.

Write the words of your letter.

Base your letter on what you have read in **Text E**, but be careful to use your own words. Address each of the three bullet points.

Start your letter, "Dearest Daughter …".

Write about 250–350 words.

 Text E: A Chinese take-away

She had come to tell them of her decision.

Standing by the door of the kitchen in the semi-darkness, a faint odour of bleach and onions greeted her like an old and comfortable companion. Silence, condensed by the hum of the refrigerators, echoed through and drew her in.

The florescent strips flickered before exploding off the hard, sharp surfaces, pricking out the edges, threatening the shadows. This was a kitchen that spoke not of home and its comforts but of forges, armoury and battle. For now, the steel rested. The oil in the deep fryer was cool, brown and thick as treacle. The heavy iron range* stood dominating the room like an altar;

A war zone on Friday nights

the four holes cut side by side into its black metal looked curiously vulnerable to her, and she resisted the temptation to cover them up with the woks that huddled upside down like turtles beneath the range.

Daughter was thoughtful and protective (not aggressive)

She walked across the room to the chopping board that stood on its own. Knives and choppers of different shapes and sizes hung from one of its edges, resembling a set of monstrous teeth. She could almost hear the thud of a heavy blade cleaving through flesh and bone onto the wood below. Delicately, she traced the scars on the surface. Tiny fragments of wood tickled her fingertips. In two hours her mother would come down the stairs and enter this arena. The fires would be lit, the oil would begin to bubble and steam and the steel would start to clash. She remembered Friday nights when she was a child. Friday was the busiest night of the week. People invaded the take-away in hordes after the pubs had closed [and] demanded to be fed. Inside the kitchen she would sit, unable to help: the still centre in the madly spinning wheel of movement around her. She would look backwards and forwards between her father and her mother. Their faces frightened her, she could not recognise them. They were not their daytime selves, they became something impersonal, mechanical, and even monstrous. They were like the knives, slashing, paring, chopping, slicing, dividing. Moving through the thick greasy white smoke like the warriors of old, advancing in the mists of dawn; they looked invincible. Every ounce of being was consumed in the task of making food. It could not be called "cooking". Cooking sounded too homely. No, like alchemists, they brought forth food out of steel and fire. Their creations subdued and sated the hungry hordes that bayed impatiently outside.

Daughter is gentle and sensitive

Like a medieval war

Customers as invaders

Daughter used to sit in middle of kitchen looking helpless and frightened – we were too busy to go to her

We (parents) became other people

Sound of knives

Daughter said preparing food in this kitchen was not like home-cooking

Our (parents') food quietened angry, noisy people ("hordes" = Tartars/Ghengis Khan?). She didn't feel she could do this every week – too stressful and physically demanding

She walked over and bent down to pick up one of the steel woks beneath the range. She tested it for its weight, savouring the way it felt to grip the wooden handle in her hand and the tension stretching her wrist. She dropped it onto one of the holes and it made a dull clunk as it landed. She walked round and round the kitchen, circling the aluminium worktop that was the centrepiece of the room. At times, she would stride, eyes wide and blazing. Then at other times her steps turned into a shuffle. She sighed and muttered, shaking her head: *I can't, I can't do it, I can't, I really can 't. They can. But not me. I'm too soft: too weak, too split. I don't have it - what it takes. I will fail.*

But there was another voice in her head, saying: *you can, you can do it. Of course you can. You have had the training. You have the guts. You have stamina. That's all you need. The rest will take care of itself.* She heard footsteps. She felt a shaking in the depths of her stomach. They would ask her and she would not know what to say [but] she could not stay and work in the kitchen.

You saw her in the kitchen that day and understood her dilemma – wanting to be part of family business but not being suited to it

* **iron range** cooking oven and hobs

It is important to be able to create topic sentences from the bullet points given in Question 3 as these will help you to organise your response well. Organising compositions around topic sentences will also help you in the Directed Writing task on Paper 2 and Assignment 1 in Component 3.

Apply

1 Look below at how the same student planned his answer to Question 3 using the bullet points. Do you agree with this basic content? Is there more to be included or interpreted from the text? If so, write your notes here:

....

....

....

....

....

....

....

2 Reword the bullet points so each one forms a topic sentence for the letter.

....

....

....

....

....

....

....

3 Use a spider diagram or mind map, and your topic sentences, to plan your answer here:

4 Write your answer to Question 3 on a sheet of paper.

5 You can mark your answer using the marking guide for Paper 1 Question 3 on page 202.

- What she used to do when she was a child and you were busy in the kitchen
- Busy in kitchen – you (daughter) used to sit in middle watching us/looked frightened/too many customers to take any notice of you/no place for a child/ dangerous too
- What it used to be like on Friday nights
- Hundreds of people/pushing in the queue/we were like machines cutting veg and frying/greasy smoke in clothes
- The reasons she gave for not wanting to join us in the business
- You've (daughter) had a good education/too sensitive for this work/quite understand wanting to leave/find a more peaceful place to live and work

Activity

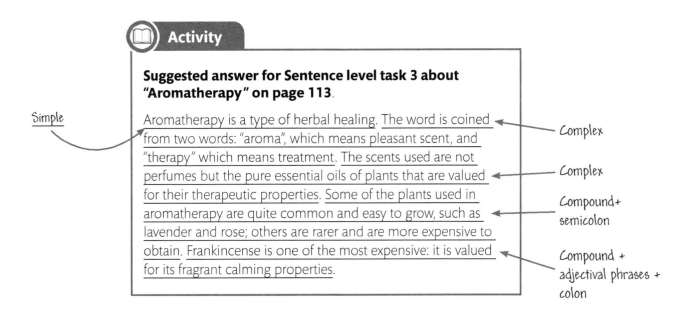

Suggested answer for Sentence level task 3 about "Aromatherapy" on page 113.

Simple

Aromatherapy is a type of herbal healing. The word is coined from two words: "aroma", which means pleasant scent, and "therapy" which means treatment. The scents used are not perfumes but the pure essential oils of plants that are valued for their therapeutic properties. Some of the plants used in aromatherapy are quite common and easy to grow, such as lavender and rose; others are rarer and are more expensive to obtain. Frankincense is one of the most expensive: it is valued for its fragrant calming properties.

Complex

Complex

Compound+ semicolon

Compound + adjectival phrases + colon

Review

Take a few minutes to think about your word and sentence grammar skills, then fill out the table below to assess your progress so far.

	Rather poor	Average	Good	Excellent
My vocabulary is …				
My use of different sentence structures is …				
I can identify topic sentences in a text				
I can create topic sentences for my paragraphs				
My summary skills are …				
Further thoughts and concerns				
My current progress for Paper 1 is …				

Raise your grade

Now make notes on what you can do to raise your grade.

I can read more efficiently by...	
I can improve my language skills at word level by ...	
I can improve my language skills at sentence level by ...	
I can write a better summary by ...	
I can understand the writer's craft better by ...	
In Question 1 I need to ...	
In Question 2 I need to ...	
In Question 3 I need to	
My target grade for Paper 1 is now ...	

Objectives

In this unit you will:

- Review your composition writing skills
- Explore the use of narrative voice and emotive language
- Practise planning compositions
- Practise writing descriptive and narrative compositions
- Review your progress and how to raise your grade

Depending on which component you are doing, you have to write compositions in Paper 2 – Writing and in Component 3 – Coursework Portfolio. In Paper 2 Section B, you will be asked to write either a descriptive or a narrative composition. Alternatively, you need to write a descriptive composition for Assignment 2 *and* a narrative composition for Assignment 3 for your portfolio.

> In Paper 2 and Component 3, you need to show how well you:
>
> - articulate experience and express what you think, feel and imagine
> - organise and structure ideas and opinions for a deliberate effect
> - use a range of vocabulary and sentence structures for style
> - use register appropriate to the context of your composition
> - make accurate use of spelling, punctuation and grammar.

 Activity

Section B: Composition

Answer **one** question from Section B.

Write about 350–450 words on **one** of the following questions.

Up to 16 marks are available for the content and structure of your answer, and up to 24 marks for the style and accuracy of your writing.

EITHER

Descriptive Writing

2   Describe a holiday resort or tourist spot at a quiet time.

OR

Descriptive Writing

3   Imagine you have just started a job in a café or restaurant. Describe the place, its customers, and your thoughts and feelings as you do your work.

Narrative Writing

4   "The figure in the long, black coat." Use this as the title of a narrative.

OR

Narrative Writing

5   Write a story that starts with the opening of a door to a room that you are not supposed to enter.

What examiners are looking for

If you can identify what makes a good descriptive and a good narrative composition (like an examiner), you are already part way to improving and developing your creative writing skills. First, recap on what you know.

Apply

1 What is the difference between a narrative composition and a descriptive composition?

A narrative composition is ....

....

A descriptive composition is ....

....

2 Write down the title of your favourite short story or novel and say why you like it.

My favourite story/novel is ....

I like it because ....

....

Now assess some sample compositions and explore what examiners are looking for in descriptive and narrative compositions.

Apply

1 Read, then keyword, the exam-style question on the previous page.

2 Read the four sample compositions on the following pages. Two are descriptive compositions in response to Question 2; the other two are narrative compositions in response to Question 4. Decide which composition is stronger and which is weaker in each category. You can write notes in the margin if you wish, but sum up your comments on the content, structure, style and accuracy in the table after each composition.

3 Compare your comments with the examiner comments for each composition on pages 141–42.

Student A: Question 2 (Descriptive Writing)

A holiday resort at a quiet time

"Out of season" they call it, when the café's are closed and the beach hut's are empty. This is the time of year I like beast because we get the beach just for us. My friends and me go down on the beach at weekend and play beach volleyball or just mess around. Even when it's rough and there's rain or a strom we go down to the beach and have a good a time. When I was little I like picking up shells and makeing patterns and sometimes when I found some wood or rope I'd make a sort of picture in the sand. Nowadays we hang out under the peer. It's a bit smelly and there's usually rotten fish or dead bird's there but we don't mind. Under the pier out of season you can hear what people are saying up above sometimes which is funny sometimes and makes us laugh. Sometimes we make weird noises and people think the peer is haunted and run away. Mostly though there's just us and we tell wierd stories and that makes us laugh though sometimes I don't like it because my friend's can be crule.

Out of season along the front it's quiet in winter. Sometimes there's not many people because the weather's so bad and you have to push against the wind. It's good though because you can ride a bike along the front and nobody tells you not to or moans at you for getting in there way.

In winter the people with businuses on the front paint there kiosks and do repairs. Sometimes you can smell the paint and creosote that they use to keep the seawater out of the wood of their kiosks. The ice-cream parlour always gets a new paint in winter and every year it's a different colour. Last year it was lime green. The ice-cream parlor is always full in summer. Allot of people go there because it's got the best ice-cream in the area although there's lots of other ice-cream places as well. Most people don't like eating ice-cream in winter but I do. It's bit weird because cold icecream can make your mouth burn.

Even when it's out of season the sea front is a good place to be in winter without all the people. It's got a sense of ~~freedom and~~ space with the big wave's crashing in and seagull's always making ~~there~~ their baby-crying sounds that give me goosebumbs sometimes. (408 words)

Student A	
Content	
Structure	
Style	
Accuracy	
Overall effect of the composition	
What Student A could do to improve	

Student B: Question 2 (Descriptive Writing)

A holiday resort at a quiet time

What a difference a month makes! In August you can't see the sand for roasting bodies, by late September you can run the length of the beach with a kite. Except this particular beach in Holland is never really unpopulated. Even in the depths of winter there are people here, taking the air getting some much needed oxygen away from stuffy livingrooms. And on Sunday mornings there are regiments of strollers. People ~~arriving~~ walk up the beach on the right and back down on the other side. I've never seen anyone actually give directions but that's what everyone does. A quiet, Sunday morning stroll under strict, unspoken rules.

There are no rules for the weather, though. Except that you know it's going to be bitterly cold; that the wind will rip through whatever jacket you wear. ~~A day like this This~~ This, to my mind is the best time of year. The North sea can be grey in summer, but in winter it turns the colour of lead, ~~a sort of~~ greenish black. It gives the sensation of heaviness and danger. The sea pounds the beach, hammering it into submission – preventing even the most hardy tourist from stepping on its terrain. The sea own the land in winter. Crowding it with grey-green water and white foaming waves, then pulling away to observe its effect.

Further along from this beach there are sand dunes. The dunes in summer are full of nesting tourists turning pink then ~~red then racing for then~~ migrating home for the winter. While there away the dunes moves. The sand wriggles around under autumn breezes, but while everyone is tucked up away from the bad weather the dunes come to life: they shift, they change, they become other shapes. The beach isn't quiet, even in winter it is alive, in control ~~of its in its~~ of its private domain.

Take a walk along the sea front at Scheveningen, when the tourists are back in ~~their~~ offices and the children bent over there their desks – take a walk and breath in the sense of freedom, but know you are just a very small being in a powerful world. This resort never has a quiet time. (353 words)

Student B	
Content	
Structure	
Style	
Accuracy	
Overall effect of the composition	
What Student B could do to improve	

Student C: Question 4 (Narrative Writing)

The figure in the long, black coat

Every morning I used to get the 7 fifteen train to get into the city were I went to school. Some mornings ther'ed be a man sitting farther up the top floor carrage wearing a long black cloak. I couldn't see that it was long when he was sitting down but we got off at the same stop and then I could see that it was down to the ground. I never took much notice. I thought he was some middle-aged goth or perhaps worked for a funeral firm or something. ~~To be honest~~ I didn't think about him at all until one day I saw him go into a door I'd never noticed before in a wall not far from our school.

The wall covered in graffiti but boring stuff not pictures or a clever message or anything like that. But after this I started to wonder what was behind the door if it was a house or warehouse or workshop or maybe a funeral place. I got really curious and it started to bother me during the day during lessons. I started to doodle pictures of the door and the man and sometimes I'd draw them together.

I had to know what was behind that door and why the man was wearing the long ~~cloak~~ coat so I started to watch out for him on the train. One day I plucked up courage and sat behind him. He smelled like my grandmother's wardrobe mothballs make that sort of smell. So I decided he kept his coat in a place like my grandma's cupboard. But he didn't look old from the back anyway. He wore an old fashioned hat like in gangster movies so I got to thinking that what was behind the door was like in the old gangster movies a sort of ~~taverna~~ club with old cars and jazz.

Today I found out.

I got off the train right behind him and followed him as close as I could and then when he opened the door which ᵂᵃˢ ~~didn't even have a lock I noticed but~~ just a proped up house door with ~~not hinjes~~ without hinges. ~~He went through the door and it~~ ᵀʰᵉ ᵖˡᵃᶜᵉ was full of stuffed animals. Some were in glass casses and some were on bits of wood and everywhere had a bad smell ~~that I think might have been~~ ˡⁱᵏᵉ formaldehide for preserving dead things.

I stopped dead in my tracks. My whole skin shivvered.

And then he turned round this ~~man~~ figure in the long black coat and I could see he'd got marbles instead of eyes.

So I turned round and ran! (414 words)

Student C	
Content	
Structure	
Style	
Accuracy	
Overall effect of the composition	
What Student C could do to improve	

Student D: Question 4 (Narrative Writing)

The figure in the long, black coat

The figure in the long black coat was on the edge of her vision. "Don't be silly," Jessie said to herself.

"What's the matter, Gran?" Stephie asked, his her eyes looking up at her worried.

"Nothing," Jess said. This was the way movies started. It's raining and someone sees a figure on the other side of the graveyard, someone they haven't seen for a long time and then you find out who it is. Except in this case Jessie knew exactly who it was. It was her husband and he had died and was in the grave.

Later, while everyone was eating cake and drinking lemon tea or orange-aid Stevie came up to her and said, "Who was it Gran. The man in the long black coat."

Jessie shook her head. "Tell me," Stephie insisted. "It's someone you know. Who?"

"All right. Come and sit down and I'll tell you all about him."

Stephie and her grandmother went to sit in the garden. When they were sitting down two of Stephie's cousins came and joined them.

Afraid her gran wouldn't tell her story with them there Stephie tried to get rid of them but they weren't shifting so she said, "Tell us all Gran, about the man in the long black coat."

Jessie looked at her ^grandchildren and they became ~~not little~~ her friends and it was half a century ago. They were waiting in line to see a fortune-teller at the carnival. Jessie didn't want to go in but her friends wanted to know who they were going to meet and who they were going to marry. ~~and~~ Jessie thought it was all a lot of nonsense but she went along anyway.

The fortune-teller was one of the cleaningladies at her school in a headscarf with bells on it. Jessie wanted to laugh but then it was her turn and suddenly she felt afraid.

"You will meet a tall, dark stranger in a long black coat," the fortune-teller cleaninglady said.

Afterward they all giggled, specially Jessie because where they lived the temperature in winter didn't even go down to 15 degrees ^celcius so nobody ever wore a coat, and never a long black one.

But when she got home her father was standing in the kitchen with a letter. "I'm being sent to England he said."

"That's great news," Jessie mother said, "because now our daughter can go to Oxford or Cambridge."

~~Five~~ Three years later Jessie was ~~in a queue at college~~ on her way to return her library books and she saw a boy standing across the hall: he was tall, dark and handsome and wearing a long black coat down to the floor.

"And that was your grandpa," Jessie said to her audience. (448 words)

Student D	
Content	
Structure	
Style	
Accuracy	
Overall effect of the composition	
What Student D could do to improve	

 Examiner comments

Student A: Question 2 (Descriptive Writing)
Total: 16/40 marks

Student makes some attempt to articulate personal experience of what is thought, felt and imagined. The composition has some structure but lacks planning for a deliberate effect. Vocabulary is limited, with numerous repetitions. Register is appropriate to the context. Grammar is basically sound but spelling is poor (misuse of the apostrophe in plurals) and should have been corrected. Overall, there is a lack of style or attempt to create an atmosphere other than a general retelling of personal experience.

Content: 5/16 marks

The content is simple, and ideas and events limited. The structure is partially organised but limited in its effect. Descriptive composition: includes recording of some relevant events with limited detail.

Style and accuracy: 11/24 marks

Basic vocabulary and a range of straightforward sentence structures. Register shows awareness of the context. Frequent errors in spelling, punctuation and grammar, occasionally serious.

 Examiner comments

Student B: Question 2 (Descriptive Writing)
Total: 37/40 marks

An excellent piece including well-articulated personal experience of what is thought, felt and imagined. The composition is structured and has been thought through for its overall effect. Vocabulary is sophisticated and figurative language used effectively. Grammar is sound, with a few minor spelling mistakes possibly due to exam conditions. Overall, a stylish attempt to create atmosphere with some sophisticated comments on human behaviour and the environment.

Content: 15/16 marks

The content is complex, engaging and effective. The structure is secure, well balanced, carefully managed for effect. Descriptive composition: Many well-defined and developed ideas and images create a convincing overall picture with varieties of focus.

Style and accuracy: 22/24 marks

Precise, well-chosen vocabulary and varied sentence structures, chosen for effect. Consistent well-chosen register suitable for the context. Spelling, punctuation and grammar are almost always accurate.

Examiner comments

Student C: Question 4 (Narrative Writing)

Total: 20/40 marks

Despite the spontaneous nature of the narrative, it is intended to be entertaining and creates some elements of tension. There is a discernible, relevant plot and some structure (borrowing from the other question on the paper). The composition is generally cohesive, with some narrative features such as characterisation and setting of scene.

Content: 9/16 marks

The content is relevant with some development (misuse of "cloak" is corrected to "coat"). The structure is competently managed although there is little evidence of planning.

Style and accuracy: 11/24 marks

Vocabulary is simple and there is a range of straightforward sentence structures. Register is appropriate for the context. Frequent errors of spelling, punctuation and grammar, occasionally serious.

 Examiner comments

Student D: Question 4 (Narrative Writing)

Total: 26/40 marks

A fairly sophisticated and ambitious story with convincing content and sound plot structure. The narrative progresses effectively to the conclusion but change in point of view hinders success. Sentences are varied for effect. Despite narrative voice shift, student has made an ambitious attempt to write a convincing short story.

Content: 9/16 marks

The content is developed, engaging and effective. The structure is relatively well managed, although there is a shift in point of view that may not have been planned. The plot is defined and developed (under exam conditions) with features of fiction writing such as description, characterisation, a basic framing device and a climax.

Style and accuracy: 17/24 marks

Vocabulary is mostly precise and a range of sentence structures are used for effect. Register and style are appropriate for the context. Some images are successfully used for deliberate effect. Spelling, punctuation and grammar are mostly accurate, with occasional minor errors.

Improving your composition writing skills

A good way to start planning a narrative or descriptive composition is to consider three main points:

- **Who will be reading the composition** Have a target reader in mind. This will help you decide on the content and tone of your composition. There is a big difference, for example, between a children's fantasy story and an adult crime novel, between travel writing and a scientist's autobiography. The examiner should be able to identify your target reader through your style and use of language.

- **Who is telling the story or giving the description** Decide whether you will write in the first or the third person, as each will have a different impact on your composition.
- **How is the story/description being told** The examiner comments on pages 141–42 identified some successful ways of "telling" a story or description. You can also explore the use of emotive language below and on pages 144–45.

Narrative voice

In a first-person narrative, the story is told from the narrator's point of view using "I" and "we". We usually know if the narrator is male or female and, if relevant, the writer lets us know the narrator's age, ethnic background and other details that might influence how they see the world or experience events. In a story (not a personal account), the narrative voice is that of a fictitious persona.

In a third-person narrative, we do not know who is telling the story. It may be the writer but, alternatively, they may have adopted a persona to tell the story. The writer may use an omniscient narrator, who knows everything that is happening in the plot and what characters are thinking. This type of narrator describes scenes and what is happening without making judgmental comments or voicing opinions.

First- and third-person narrators both use two major techniques: show and tell.

- The writer shows people's characters through what they say and do, how they speak and how they react to one another. Readers also learn about the past and the future from what characters say.
- The writer tells us about the characters through description and setting, including what they look like, where they are and what is happening to them.

An omniscient third-person narrator can also tell readers what characters are thinking. The writer:

- shows what a character is thinking through a kind of inner speech called free indirect thought (e.g. Is it over yet?)
- tells what a character is thinking through direct thought (e.g. "Is it over yet," he wondered.)

Emotive language

A very good way to improve your narrative and descriptive writing is to draw your reader in by using emotive language to create a particular effect, especially in the opening scene.

 Link

You can read more about point of view and narrative voice in Unit 3 of the *Complete First Language English for Cambridge IGCSE® Student Book*.

 **QuestionRecap**

Emotive language includes words and phrases that affect the reader's emotions and/or attitudes.

Apply

Look at the following openings from successful stories for adults and children, a memoir and travel writing. Try to identify what makes each extract so effective. You can write notes on each extract. Try to:

a Identify a hook. What word or phrase will make the reader want to read on?

b Identify the writer's use of emotive or affective language. How does the opening make you feel?

I was set down from the carrier's cart at the age of three; and there with a sense of bewilderment and terror my life in the village began.

The June grass, amongst which I stood, was taller than I was, and I wept. I had never been so close to grass before. It towered above me and all around me, each blade tattooed with tiger-skins of sunlight. It was knife-edged, dark, and a wicked green, thick as a forest and alive with grasshoppers that chirped and chattered and leapt through the air like monkeys.

I was lost and didn't know where to move.

From *Cider with Rosie*, a memoir by Laurie Lee (1959)

I have never told you any of this before – I have never told anyone, and indeed, writing it down and sealing it up in an envelope to read at some future date may still not count as "telling". But I shall feel better for it, I am sure of that. Now it has all come back to me, I do not want to let it go again, I must set it down.

From *Farthing House*, a short story by Susan Hill (1992)

Imagine, if you can, a small room, hexagonal in shape, like the cell of a bee. It is lighted neither by window nor by lamp, yet it is filled with a soft radiance. There are no apertures for ventilation, yet the air is fresh. There are no musical instruments, and yet, at the moment that my meditation opens, this room is throbbing with melodious sounds. An armchair is in the centre, by its side a reading-desk – that is all the furniture. And in the armchair there sits a swaddled lump of flesh – a woman, about five feet high, with a face as white as a fungus. It is to her that the little room belongs.

From *The Machine Stops*, a short story by E.M. Forster (1909)

Coraline discovered the door a little while after they moved into the house.

It was a very old house – it had an attic under the roof and a cellar under the ground and an overgrown garden with huge trees in it.

Coraline's family didn't own all of the house, it was too big for that. Instead they owned part of it. […]

The day after they moved in, Coraline went exploring.

She explored the garden. It was a big garden: at the very back was an old tennis court, but no one in the house played tennis and the fence around the court had holes in it and the net had mostly rotted away; there was an old rose garden, filled with stunted flyblown rose bushes; there was a rockery that was all rocks; there was a fairy ring, made of squidgy brown toadstools which smelled terrible if you accidentally trod on them.

There was also a well. On the first day Coraline's family moved in Miss Spink and Miss Forcible made a point of telling Coraline how dangerous the well was, and they warned her to be sure she kept away from it. So Coraline set off to explore for it […]

From *Coraline*, a novella for children by Neil Gaiman (2002)

"It's curious," said Joyce Lemprière, "but I hardly like telling you my story. It happened a long time ago – five years ago to be exact – but it's sort of haunted me ever since. The smiling, bright, top part of it – and the hidden gruesomeness underneath […]

From *The Bloodstained Pavement*, a short story by Agatha Christie (1932)

The coup began at seven on Sunday morning. It was a grey and windless dawn and the grey Atlantic rollers broke in long even lines along the beach. The palms above the tidemark shivered in a current of cooler air that blew in off the breakers. Out at sea – beyond the surf – there were several black fishing canoes. Buzzards were circling above the market, swooping now and then to snatch up scraps of offal. The butchers were working, even on a Sunday.

From *A Coup*, travel writing by Bruce Chatwin (1983)

Practising your creative writing skills

Combine what you have learned above to write your own gripping opening to a story.

 Apply

Create a gripping opening for this Narrative Writing question:

Write a story that starts with the opening of a door to a room that you are not supposed to enter.

....

....

....

....

....

....

Exam tip

Descriptive and narrative compositions both require convincing content and an effective structure (paragraphing), which involves not only your writing skills but also your thinking skills.

Planning compositions

Knowing that examiners will be assessing the content and structure, style and accuracy of your writing can help when you are planning your composition. Look at how a successful student started planning a descriptive writing assignment about underground railway journeys for Component 3.

QuestionRecap

Mood and tone are created through the writer's choice of words. In fiction, and many types of non-fiction, how the writer describes locations and images contributes to how the reader perceives those places, people/characters and/or events. Mood and tone are created through combinations of:

- interesting or unusual diction
- the rhythm of the language used
- sounds created by alliteration or sibilance
- use of imagery.

Content (where/who/why) Structure (leading to conclusion)	Style and use of English
Include what I:	Include:
• think	• see
• feel	• hear
• imagine.	• smell
	• taste
Plan for topic sentences:	• touch.
• Intro – where and what	Create sense of being underground and on a train through mood and tone
• What – Tube/Metro	
• Where – city centres	
• Who – commuters	
• Why – work not pleasure	
• My thoughts, opinion and feelings	
• Conclusion	

Lists and tables are good ways to plan but if you are a more visual person you might prefer to use mind maps or spider diagrams for planning.

Mind maps

Mind mapping involves writing down a central idea or the topic of your composition and thinking up new and/or related ideas that radiate out from the main subject. You can write in key words, interesting vocabulary and imagery, and link ideas as you go along. To make a rapid mind map in an exam situation:

- think about the main elements needed for the question
- jot down your ideas
- look for connections between the ideas
- circle and link separate points
- join ideas logically with lines
- number the points to organise them into paragraphs and reach a conclusion
- write a topic sentence for each paragraph.

Spider diagrams

Spider diagrams have the central task, subject or idea in the "body", with ideas, images and related topics attached as "legs". To make a rapid spider diagram in an exam:

- put the topic or question in the centre
- add each main point directly related to the topic as a "leg"
- add examples and related thoughts to form a web of ideas to expand each main point
- number the points to form a logical sequence for your paragraphs and reach a conclusion
- write a topic sentence for each paragraph.

✏ Apply

Choose one of the four exam-style questions for Paper 2 Section B on page 135. Use one of the planning strategies and time how long it takes you to create an effective plan.

....

....

....

....

....

....

....

....

....

....

....

....

....

Writing a narrative/descriptive composition

In Paper 2 Section B, you can choose whether to write a descriptive or a narrative composition. You have a chance of getting better marks if you choose the type of writing you like best, descriptive or narrative.

If you are doing Component 3 instead of Paper 2, you need to write a descriptive composition for Assignment 2 *and* a narrative composition for Assignment 3 for your Coursework portfolio. You can get better marks by writing several drafts and checking and rechecking your assignments to make sure they are as good as you can make them.

Narrative/descriptive composition for Paper 2 Section B

✏ Apply

Write the Paper 2 Section B composition you have just planned. Don't forget to write the number of the question and a title for your composition at the top.

....
....
....
....
....
....
....
....
....
....
....
....
....
....
....
....
....
....
....
....
....
....

(If you need more space, write on an extra sheet of paper.)

Descriptive composition for Coursework Assignment 2

Read a student's descriptive writing for Assignment 2. As it is coursework, they should have written various drafts and there should be no errors in the grammar or spelling. You can see his planning on page 146.

Component 3, Assignment 2: Descriptive writing

Going underground

Living in a big city has many advantages – theatres, cinema, elegant restaurants and fast-food joints on every corner, but if you live there permanently there are a number of disadvantages, specially the traffic and congestion. This can make getting to work or getting to school a daily risk. Will we make it in time? Will we be late again? Will we even make it in one piece?

For this reason, I started using the underground train, called the metro where we live. The metro in Stockholm is clean and efficient and has none of the risks of trying to get from one island to another over narrow, traffic-jammed bridges. The city planners have even tried to make it more interesting by decorating the walls of some stations so it looks as if you're going down into a cave. But once you've noticed this once, you stop seeing it and it's as if you're doing the journey blind because you know all the stops and even get to know some of the faces of the people you see every day waiting to be taken from one place to another.

These people, like me, know the route so well – and there's nothing to look at out of the window – so, like me they go into a sort of comma or light sleeping condition. Those lucky enough to get a seat nod off. Their heads nod down over their chins until be some peace of human magic they wake up just before their stop and get out. Those who have to stand try to balance their backs against a bar or central metal pilar and they too go into a semi-comatose state. There's always a few gossiping on their phones, but on the out route – going to work or school – not so many people are talking to themselves via piece of smart plastic.

It's curious that some stations in Stockholm have cavern-like cladding because tunnels feature in Norse mythology quite a lot. In our ancient myths and legends clever dwarves forged swords and precious objects underground in caves. Dragons lived in caves as well, sleeping on piles of gold. You won't see any swords or precious gold on my journeys through Scandinavian tunnels though. Quite the opposite. Most people seem to wear black or dowdy colours; there's nothing bright except the electric light in the train.

One of the effects of being underground and half-asleep is that your sense of smell wakes up. I can more or less tell where we are when the doors slide open and there's a blast of air that comes whistling down the escalator. The oldest parts of town have a rubbery smell. Then, when you leave the train and go up towards the entrance to the station there are other smells such as the pop corn machine in a convenience store, or the smell of fresh bread from a bakery. But these are the good smells, most of the other odours are to do with damp, underground walls and traffic fumes that get trapped inside at street level.

Getting out of a train during the morning rush hour has its risks too, though. Not as bad as travelling by car or bus, but there's always the risk that the crowd trying to get into the train won't let you off. My worst nightmare was being trapped on the underground going round and round the system all day and all night. In Norse mythology the supreme god Odin banished the evil giantess Hel to "the world beneath the worlds". It's no mystery to me that Hell is underground. What a way to start the day. (607 words)

✏️ **Apply**

Look at the marking guide for Component 3 Assignment 2 on page 206 and decide how well this student has performed against the assessment objectives.

Content and structure	
Style and accuracy	
This student could improve the composition by …	

Narrative composition for Coursework Assignment 3

If you do not feel creative enough to write a fictional story for Assignment 3, consider writing a first-person account of a real situation instead. This style of writing is found in autobiographies, diaries/journals and magazine articles.

 QuestionRecap

Writing accounts

Accounts inform and entertain to retell past events. When you write an account of a past experience:

- start with a short sentence to grab the reader's attention
- then set the scene: who, where, when
- retell the events in chronological order – what happened and when
- focus on specific events, objects or people
- use the past tense and first-person active voice
- use time connectives (e.g. meanwhile, after that, much later, almost immediately)
- use interesting words to engage the reader
- use imagery and metaphors so the reader understands what you saw, felt, heard, etc.
- link the final paragraph back to the opening lines
- finish with a meaningful comment but not a rhetorical question.

 Apply

Read the first-person account on the next page of a real event written for a popular magazine. The writer recounts her experience of flying in a motorised paraglider alongside swans. Using the list on writing accounts above, annotate the text to identify what the writer has done well. In particular, look at how she has organised her material and how she includes her thoughts and feelings.

Text A: Silence

"I loved every perilous and beautiful moment."

To conquer her fear of flying, Sacha Dench embarked upon an epic journey, witnessing the world from a bird's eye view.

As the sun was rising, a pink light skimmed the clouds. I was flying over northern Russia. The land below was too cold for trees; just vast frozen plains as far as I

5 could see. I was braving temperatures of −25° in a motorised paraglider to follow the migration path of swans. It was a journey that had been years in the planning, requiring courage that had taken many

10 more years to muster.

A childhood admiration for David Attenborough led to my career in conservation. It took me around the world studying turtles, sharks and pollution. It

15 also led to a near-death experience when a six-seater plane I was travelling in was engulfed in a thunderstorm.

It was a terrifying experience that left me with a chronic fear of flying. I knew nothing

20 about flight, and I realised in order to conquer this fear I would need to immerse myself in it. So I started paragliding. For my first few flights I insisted on flying tandem with a trainer. But it wasn't in my nature to

25 let fear win. Gradually, my fear gave way to exhilaration.

A new job with the Wildfowl and Wetlands Trust led to my interest in Bewick swans, a species in decline. Something about

30 these graceful creatures took hold in my heart. I decided to join them in the skies in a motorised paraglider, to follow their migration path from Russia, over eastern Europe, over the English Channel, all the

35 way to Gloucestershire. I would track their progress, talk to locals, and raise awareness of their plight.

In September last year I started my journey. I would be accompanied by a team, but I

40 would be alone in the sky, with only the swans for company.

Flying is like entering an alternative reality; disorientating, mesmerising, liberating. Nothing could have prepared me for the

45 spectacular sight of the changing landscape from the sky, the swirling colours, the winding rivers. At one point, a flock of geese flew with me in formation, tucking in as if I were the lead bird. And during

50 a nasty patch of fog, I circled up above the clouds into the sunny peacefulness to discover flocks of swans all over my horizon. It was pure magic.

Three months into my trip, as I flew

55 towards Calais, the White Cliffs of Dover came into view. Emotion overtook me and I burst into tears. I had loved every perilous and beautiful moment, and didn't want the trip to end, but those famous cliffs seemed

60 to be smiling at me, reminding me it was time to come home.

Flying is like entering a new reality …

Nothing could have prepared me for it.

From *Good Housekeeping* magazine,
1 May 2017

QuestionRecap

The advantage of writing a first-person account is that you can draw on your own experiences and emotions. This will enable you to include your thoughts, feelings and ideas about a person, place or situation.

Exam tip

- Be careful not to turn this narrative composition into a descriptive one.
- Although this is narrative writing, you still need to create a mood or tone, so use imagery and interesting language.
- Ensure you have a clear beginning, middle and end.
- Use dialogue to show what is happening and interior monologue to convey your thoughts.

 Apply

You may not have had such a wonderful experience as Sacha Dench's flight with swans but you may have done something that has changed your life, views or attitudes in some way. Choose one of the following topics or one of your own. Plan and then write a first-person account of 500–800 words for Component 3 Assignment 3 in the space provided.

1 First day at school or first day in a new school
2 Getting stuck up a tree
3 Being caught doing something you shouldn't
4 Riding a horse, bicycle or camel in a race or competition
5 Getting lost in a city or forest
6 A pleasant or unpleasant memory
7 Visiting a museum
8 Hiking across mountains or moorland
9 A road trip across an unpopulated landscape

(If you need more space, write on an extra sheet of paper.)

Review

Take a few minutes to think about what you know about writing compositions and your skills, then use the table below to review your progress so far.

"Point of view" means …	
Emotive language is …	
Using the five senses in descriptions involves …	
I enjoy creative writing because …	
I do not enjoy creative writing because …	
I prefer writing narrative compositions because …	
I prefer writing descriptive (non-fiction) compositions because …	
Further thoughts and concerns	

Raise your grade

Now make notes on what you can do to raise your grade.

I can improve the planning of my compositions by ...	
I can improve the structure of my compositions by ...	
I can improve the content of my compositions by ...	
I can improve my different writing styles by ...	
I can improve my descriptive writing by ...	
I can improve my narrative writing by ...	
My target grade for Paper 2 or Component 3 is now ...	

Objectives

In this unit you will:

- Review the skills you need for Papers 1 and 2
- Practise answering exam-style papers

- Mark your Directed Writing and Composition
- Review your progress and how to raise your grade

Practice Paper 1 – Reading

Review

Before you start reading this practice paper, take a few minutes to read through what Paper 1 is asking you to do. The exact wording of each question paper will differ because of the nature and content of the reading texts (A, B and C), but examiners will assess you on the same skills.

You will find the answers at www.oxfordsecondary.com/esg-for-caie-igcse

In Question 1, you will be asked to:

- find evidence of explicit ideas in the text
- use your own words to explain explicit ideas from the text
- identify and explain implied or inferred ideas in the text
- select relevant ideas from the text to answer the summary question
- organise and structure a summary according to a specific question
- summarise in your own words to show your understanding of the text
- write accurately using correct spelling, grammar structures and punctuation.

In Question 2, you will be asked to:

- find particular words or phrases in the text
- explain in your own words the writer's use of specific words or phrases
- use an example from the text to explain how the writer uses language for a specific effect
- explain how the writer uses language to convey meaning and create effect in words or phrases (including imagery) you have chosen from the text.

In Question 3, you will be asked to:

- adopt the point of view of a persona (take on a role) and write for a specific purpose and audience
- consider ideas in the text from that perspective (different to the point of view in the text)
- write in a particular style: letter, report, journal, speech, interview or article
- identify and use relevant ideas in the text to fully address each bullet point in the task
- use your own words fluently, accurately and clearly
- develop and extend ideas based on details implied in the text.

Read Texts A, B and C on the following pages, then answer the questions, which start on page 162. You may take as long as you wish with this practice paper, but make a note of how long each question takes you.

📖 Text A: Istanbul

The American author Bill Bryson is visiting Istanbul in Turkey.

It is the noisiest, dirtiest, busiest city I've ever seen. Everywhere there is noise – car horns tooting, sirens shrilling, people shouting, muezzins wailing, ferries on the Bosphorus sounding their booming horns. Everywhere, too, there is ceaseless activity – people pushing carts, carrying trays of food or coffee, humping huge and ungainly loads (I saw
5　one guy with a sofa on his back), people every five feet selling something: lottery tickets, wristwatches, cigarettes, replica perfumes.

　　Every few paces people come up to you wanting to shine your shoes, sell you postcards or guidebooks, lead you to their brother's carpet shop or otherwise induce you to part with some trifling sum of money. Along the Galata Bridge, swarming with pedestrians, beggars
10　and load bearers, amateur fishermen stood pulling the most poisoned-looking fish I ever hope to see from the oily waters below. At the end of the bridge two guys were crossing the street to Sirkeci Station, threading their way through the traffic leading brown bears on leashes. No one gave them a second glance. Istanbul is, in short, one of those great and exhilarating cities where almost anything seems possible. […]

15　I wandered around for a couple of hours, impressed by the tumult, amazed that in one place there could be so much activity. I walked past the Blue Mosque and Aya Sofia, peeling postcard salesmen from my sleeve as I went, and tried to go to Topkapi, but it was closed. I headed instead for what I thought was the national archaeological museum, but I somehow missed it and found myself presently at the entrance to a large, inviting and miraculously
20　tranquil park, the Gülhane. It was full of cool shade and happy families. There was a free zoo, evidently much loved by children, and somewhere a café playing Turkish […] music […].

　　At the bottom of a gently sloping central avenue, the park ended in a sudden and stunning view of the Bosphorus, glittery and blue. I took a seat at an open-air taverna,
25　ordered a Coke and gazed across the water to the white houses gleaming on the brown hillside of Üsküdar two miles across the strait. Distant cars glinted in the hot sunshine and ferries plied doggedly back and forth across the Bosphorus and on out to the distant Princes' Islands, adrift in a bluish haze. It was beautiful and a perfect place to stop.

From *Neither Here Nor There* by Bill Bryson

Text B: An American in India

An American student, Brian Gallagher, went to India on a university exchange programme. On his return he wrote an account of his experience. (This text contains American spelling, but you should answer using whichever form of spelling is natural to you.)

It would be difficult to underestimate the value of spending time in a foreign country, especially a country that is so particularly foreign to one's own – as India is to mine. Typically mundane experiences such as walking down a nondescript and common street, become the most

5 incredible adventures. Surrounded by novelty, the world is suddenly alive and fascinating. I remember very clearly my first impressions of India, and how enamored I was with everything that I saw around me. Nothing could bore me, because everything was colored with the culture of my surroundings – and what a different color it was! I was mystified

10 by the cryptic languages I saw on billboards and the towers of Hindu temples along the roadsides. I was entirely bemused by the animals in the streets, as well as all the rickshaws and the old British-style taxis that I saw everywhere. I was pleasantly amused by Indian courtesy and impressed by Indian attitudes towards marriage and the family.

15 Everything, everywhere, jumped out at my senses and engaged my mind like it could never have at home.

It was these small and everyday things that made India such a wildly different place. The extraordinary things, of course, were impressive; but they were impressive because they were extraordinary. It was

20 far more remarkable to find the merely common things that seemed extraordinary. Each one revealed either something truly singular about India, or something in my own conception of the world that had been clouded by my relatively sheltered life. And recognizing either one was incredibly mind-opening. It was by getting in touch with these common

25 differences that I was able to understand India, at least in a limited sense. By dealing one-on-one with the students and faculty at Manipal, I gained an insight into Indian character and by speaking with friends about their futures, I learned a little about Indian values and aspirations. These tiny and individual experiences eventually add up to the whole

30 that is Indian culture and while I would never pretend to comprehend that whole in its fullness, I am incredibly grateful to have come to understand a portion of it.

By Brian Gallagher, *IAESTE Annual Review*, 2007

Text C: A taxi ride in Old Shanghai

Christopher Banks is in Old Shanghai, in China, investigating the disappearance of his parents. He has learned that a key witness lives nearby. It is the 1930s, China is at war with Japan and Christopher is in a part of the city that is not safe for foreigners. (This text is slightly longer than you will get in a Text C for Paper 1.)

I got into the car and the young [taxi driver] started the engine. He turned the vehicle a full circle, then we took another narrow side-street. As we did so, many thoughts crowded into my mind at once. I wondered if I should tell the young man the significance of the journey we were making, and even considered asking if he was carrying a gun in the car – though
5   in the end I decided such an enquiry might only panic him.

We turned a corner into an alley even narrower than the one before. Then we turned again and came to a halt. I thought for a second we had reached our destination, but then realised what had made us stop. In the alleyway before us was a crowd of young boys trying to control a bewildered water-buffalo. There was some sort of altercation going
10   on between the boys, and as I watched, one of them gave the buffalo a clout on the nose with his stick. I felt a wave of alarm, remembering my mother's warnings throughout my childhood that these animals were as dangerous as any bull when riled. The creature did nothing, however, and the boys continued to argue. The young man sounded the horn several times to no avail, and finally, with a sigh, he began to reverse the vehicle back the
15   way we had come.

We took another alley nearby, but this diversion appeared to confuse my driver, for after a few more turns, he stopped and reversed again, though this time there was no obstruction. At one point, we came out on to a broader rutted mud track with dilapidated wooden shacks all along one side.

20   "Please hurry," I said. "I have very little time."

Just then a huge crashing sound shook the ground we were travelling along. The young man continued to drive steadily, but looked nervously into the distance.

"Fighting," he said. "Fighting started again."

"It sounded awfully close," I said.

25   For the next few minutes, we steered around more narrow corners and little wooden houses, blasting the horn to scatter children and dogs. Then the car came to another abrupt halt, and I heard the young man let out an exasperated sound. Looking past him, I saw the way ahead was blocked by a barricade of sandbags and barbed wire.

"We must go all the way round," he said. "No other way."

30   "But look, we must be very close now."

"Very close, yes. But road blocked, so we must go all the way round. Be patient, sir. We get there soon."

But a distinct change had entered the young man's manner.

35 His earlier assurance had faded, and now he struck me as ridiculously young to be driving a car, perhaps no more than fifteen or sixteen. For some time, we travelled through muddy, stinking streets, down more alleys where I thought we would at any moment plunge into the open gutters – but somehow the young man always managed to keep our wheels just clear of the edges. All the while, we could hear the sound of gunfire in the distance, and see people hurrying back to the safety of their houses and

40 shelters. But there were still the children and dogs, seemingly belonging to no one, running everywhere before us, oblivious to any sense of danger. At one point, as we bumped our way across the yard of some small factory, I said:

"Now look, why don't you just stop and ask the way?"

"Be patient, sir."

45 "Be patient? But you've no more idea where we're going than I have."

"We get there soon, sir."

"What nonsense. Why do you persist in this charade? […] You're lost, but you won't admit it. We've been driving now for … well, it seems like an eternity."

He said nothing and brought us out on to a mud road that climbed steeply between

50 large heaps of factory refuse. Then came another thunderous crash somewhere alarmingly near, and the young man dropped his speed to a crawl.

"Sir. I think we go back now."

"Go back? Go back where?"

"Fighting very near. Not safe here."

55 "What do you mean, the fighting' s near?" Then an idea dawned on me. […]

"You told me the house was very near. Now we're lost. We're possibly dangerously close to the war zone."

From *When We Were Orphans* by Kazuo Ishiguro

 Activity

Re-read **Text A, *Istanbul***, and then answer **Question 1 (a)–(e)**.

Question 1

(a) Give **two** examples of why Bryson thinks Istanbul is a noisy city.

- ....

  ....

- ....

  ....

[2]

(b) Using your own words, explain what the text means by:

(i) "to part with some trifling sum" (lines 8–9) ....

....

....

[2]

(ii) "impressed by the tumult" (line 15) ....

....

....

[2]

(c) Re-read paragraph 2 ("Every few paces … anything seems possible.")

Give **two** reasons why Bryson thinks "anything seems possible" in Istanbul.

*   ....

....

*   ....

....

[2]

(d) Re-read paragraph 3 ("I wandered around … music.")

(i) Identify **two** reasons Bryson found the park "inviting and miraculously tranquil".

....

....

....

....

[2]

(ii) Explain what Bryson means by "peeling postcard salesmen from my sleeve" (lines 16–17).

....

....

[2]

(e) Re-read the final paragraph ("At the bottom of … a perfect place to stop.")

Using your own words, explain why Bryson's initial attitude to Istanbul changes in the final paragraph.

....

....

....

....

[3]

Exam tip

Annotating summary tasks with two aspects

This summary task has two aspects, so use two different coloured pencils to annotate the text.

- Look for what Gallagher finds "interesting" and "different" (to his native land).
- Mark each point in the margin with an "I" (interesting) or a "D" for different.
- Number the points in the order you want to make them in your summary.

Read **Text B, *An American in India***, and then answer **Question 1(f).**

Question 1

(f) According to **Text B**, what does Gallagher find different and interesting about his new environment?

You must **use continuous writing** (not note form) and **use your own words** as far as possible.

Your summary should be no more than 120 words.

Up to 10 marks are available for the content of your answer and up to 5 marks for the quality of your writing.

....
....
....
....
....
....
....
....
....
....
....
....
....
....
....
....
....
....
....
....
....
....
....

[15]

(If you need more lines, use an extra sheet of paper. Remember to write your name and the question number at the top.)

[Total: 30]

Read **Text C, *A taxi ride in Old Shanghai***, and then answer **Question 2(a)–(d).**

Question 2

(a) Identify a word or phrase from the text that suggests the same idea as the <u>words underlined</u>:

(i) The driver reversed although <u>nothing was blocking our way</u>.

....

[1]

(ii) The car came to another <u>sudden stop</u>.

....

[1]

(iii) The driver had lost his <u>previous confidence</u>.

....

[1]

(iv) The children were <u>unaware of</u> any danger.

....

[1]

(b) Using your own words, explain what the writer means by each of the <u>words underlined</u>:

In the alleyway before us was a crowd of young boys trying to control a bewildered water-buffalo. There was some sort of <u>altercation</u> going on between the boys, and as I watched, one of them gave the buffalo a <u>clout</u> on the nose with his stick. I felt a wave of alarm, remembering my mother's warnings throughout my childhood that these animals were as dangerous as any bull when <u>riled</u>.

(i) altercation ....

[1]

(ii) clout ....

[1]

(iii) riled ....

[1]

(c) Use **one** example from the text below to explain how the writer suggests Christopher Banks' feelings during the taxi ride.

Use your own words in your explanation.

[The young taxi driver's] earlier assurance had faded, and now he struck me as ridiculously young to be driving a car, perhaps no more than fifteen or sixteen. For some time, we travelled through muddy, stinking streets, down more alleys where I thought we would at any moment plunge into the open gutters – but somehow the young man always managed to keep our wheels just clear of the edges. All the while, we could hear the sound of gunfire in the distance, and see people hurrying back to the safety of their houses and shelters.

....
....
....
....
....
....

[3]

(d) Re-read paragraphs 1–8.

- Paragraph 1 begins "I got into the car …" and is about the start of Christopher Banks' journey to the witness's home.
- Paragraph 8 ends "… a barricade of sandbags and barbed wire."

Explain how the writer uses language to convey meaning and to create effect in these paragraphs. Choose **three** examples to support your answer. Your choices should include the use of imagery.

Write about 200–300 words.

Up to 15 marks are available for the content of your answer.

....
....
....
....
....
....
....
....
....
....
....

....
....
....
....
....
....
....
....
....
....
....
....
....
....
....
....
....
....
....
....
....
....
....
....
....
....
....
....
....
....
....

[15]

(If you need more lines, use an extra sheet of paper. Remember to write your name and the question number at the top.)

[Total: 25]

Exam tip

Discussing a writer's use of the senses

Take note of how and why the writer has used different senses: sight, sound, smell and touch.

◀◀ QuestionRecap

Quoting a writer's words

- Remember not to confuse a fictional character with the writer. This story is being told in the first person by Christopher Banks, who is a fictional persona in a novel.
- Always refer to writers by their last name.

Re-read **Text C, *A taxi ride in Old Shanghai***, and then answer **Question 3.**

Question 3

You are the young driver of the taxi. That night you write an account of the day's events in your journal. You include what you remember about:

- the Englishman who wanted to go to a nearby house
- what you saw and felt during the journey
- why you wanted to turn back.

Write the words of your account.

Base your journal entry on what you have read in **Text C**, but be careful to use your own words. Address each of the three bullet points.

Write about 250–350 words.

Up to 15 marks are available for the content of your answer and up to 10 marks for the quality of your writing.

....

....

....

....

....

....

....

....

....

....

....

....

....

....

....

....

....

....

....

....

....

....

....

....

....

....

....

....

....

....

....

....

....

....

....

....

....

....

....

....

....

....

....

....

....

....

....

....

....

....

[25]

(If you need more lines, use an extra sheet of paper. Remember to write your name and the question number at the top.)

Raise your grade for Paper 1

Don't lose any marks!

- **Generally:** Don't skip a question (intending to come back to it), then forget it. Avoid this by allowing time to review your answers. Try to answer the questions in sequence because this will give you a better understanding of the text and writer's craft as you go along.
- **Question 1(f):** Don't misread the summary task or select the wrong details. Avoid this with careful keywording.
- **Question 2(d):** Make sure you discuss the writer's choice of words in enough depth in the language task.
- **Question 3:** Sometimes students run out of time, but many fail to follow the question closely.
  - Don't miss out any of the bullet points in the question. Check you have used all the bullet points in your planning, then your writing.
  - Include relevant details such as names, times and locations. They may be vital evidence to show you have fully understood the content and ideas in the text.
  - Don't lose focus and drift away from the text and/or task. Ensure that what you write is directly linked to what you have read!
  - Don't copy from the text unless told to do so. Use your own words instead.
  - Pay close attention to the role you have been given and adopt this point of view fully to show that you have understood more than just the events and obvious content of the text.
  - Write in the style requested: letter, report, journal, speech, interview or article. For example, don't lose marks by forgetting to include an interviewer's questions or to sign off a letter in role.
  - Show you have understood implicit ideas and meanings. Extend and develop what you have read.

Review

Take a few minutes to review your thoughts about doing Paper 1.

How I felt about answering the comprehension tasks in Question 1(a)–(e)	
How I felt about writing a summary for Question 1(f)	
How I felt about identifying and explaining the writer's language for Question 2	
What I need to do to improve my performance in Question 2	
What I need to do in Question 3 when I read a text from another character's point of view	

Why the bullet points are important in Question 3.	
How I can use the bullet points in a letter, report, journal, speech, interview or article	
What else I need to focus on to raise my grade in Paper 1	
My target grade for Paper 1 is now ...	

Practice Paper 2 – Directed Writing and Composition

Review

Before you start reading this practice paper, take a few minutes to read through what Paper 2 is asking you to do. Even though the exact wording of each question paper will differ because of the nature and content of the reading text(s) (A and, possibly, B), examiners will still assess you on the same skills.

In Question 1, you will be asked to:
- write in an appropriate register (to discuss, argue or persuade)
- identify relevant ideas from a text or texts to address bullet points
- evaluate information (facts and ideas) in the text(s) in your answer
- write in a particular style (text type): speech, letter, article
- organise ideas and opinions according to the task and audience
- identify and respond to implicit meanings and attitudes, opinions and bias
- demonstrate accurate use of spelling, punctuation and grammar.

In Questions 2–5, you will be asked to:

- use a title and/or task to plan relevant and interesting content ideas for a composition
- engage your reader's interest
- organise and structure your composition for a deliberate effect
- use well-chosen vocabulary and varied sentence structures for effect
- use an appropriate register for your response
- use correct spelling, punctuation and grammar
- develop a plot for a narrative composition that includes description, characterisation and convincing details, **OR**
- write a description that contains a convincing overall picture with varieties of focus and interesting imagery.

Read Text A on the following pages, then answer the questions, which start on page 173. You may take as long as you wish, but make a note of how long each question takes you.

Text A: Sleep and the school day

This article is on sleep and the teenage brain. It comes from an online news source written by experts in different fields.

Throughout the course of our lives, our sleep patterns and the amount of sleep we need change. Babies sleep between 16 and 18 hours per day, but this is reduced to approximately seven to eight hours for an average adult. Teenagers tend to require about nine hours of sleep per night to maintain alertness, and adolescents spend more time in deep sleep than adults.

5   This knowledge has led to suggestions that delaying the time at which teenagers start school each morning could help them to learn more effectively.

Sleep is an active state, which is thought to be important for restoration and recovery of the body, fighting infection, energy conservation, memory consolidation, brain development and the experience of emotions while dreaming. It is regulated by two distinct processes. The first,

10   our "circadian pacemaker" or "biological clock" is regulated by genes, hormones and neural pathways in response to light and other external cues. The second, "homeostatic" process, reflects an individual's need for sleep or desire to stay awake.

Circadian rhythms change during puberty, probably due to hormonal changes. This results in adolescents displaying a delayed circadian sleep phase with a preference for going to bed late

15   and getting up later than adults.

In some people there may be an extreme delay in the circadian rhythm, which may be the result of a condition known as delayed sleep phase disorder. In a recent study the prevalence of this disorder in Norwegian high school children was found to be 8.4% and was associated with lower school grades, smoking and the use of stimulant drinks, plus elevated levels of anxiety and depression.

20   Public awareness of the need for adequate sleep both for adults and children is increasing and yet adolescents still don't sleep enough. Lack of sleep is associated with a number of adverse health outcomes, including obesity. A lack of sleep affects the hormones that control appetite and also disrupts glucose control. Sleep loss and associated daytime sleepiness may also contribute to the severe or fatal accidents that occur to otherwise healthy young people.

25   In children, a lack of sleep is associated with poor memory consolidation, an inability to solve complex problems and poor school performance.

In adolescents, poor academic performance and behaviour problems may arise from a lack of synchrony between their circadian biology and schools' start times. Teenagers often report shorter time in bed because of the need to wake-up early on school days – as compared with

30   weekends, when they can sleep on naturally.

Proposals to adapt the school day with a later morning start and a later finish is likely to meet the needs of the majority of students, although there will be some individual variation. It will allow them to attend school at the time when they are "biologically" more likely to maximise their learning experience. It may also decrease stress and improve problematic behaviour.

35   A number of lifestyle factors, however, also cause daytime sleepiness in children and adolescents. Apart from insufficient sleep, these include not having a regular bedtime, eating late, and using electronic gadgets late in the evening. If an individual is subjected to bright light at night, particularly blue light from electronic devices, melatonin levels are suppressed. As a result, our biological clock thinks it is daytime and there is an increase in alertness. This

40   activity is often accompanied by the consumption of caffeinated and sugary drinks, which also contribute to the inability to sleep well.

Further studies are required to generate the evidence for a change in the school day. The delayed circadian sleep phase appears in teenagers but disappears in adults so it is necessary to determine for which age group a delayed school start is most appropriate, and what the
45   optimum delay time would be for each year group. Schools will have to take into account the effect this might have on teachers, who may well be early risers. Parents also need to be consulted as starting the school day later could significantly affect their work schedules and daily routines.

Adapted from "Explainer: Why does the teenage brain need more sleep?" by Michelle A. Miller and Francesco Cappuccio

 Activity

Read **Text A, *Sleep and the school day***, and then answer **Section A, Question 1.**
Section A: Directed Writing

Question 1

Your school is conducting an enquiry into the advantages and disadvantages of changing the start of the school day. You have read about the connection between adolescents' sleep patterns and the case for delaying the start of the school day.

Write a letter to your school principal outlining why your school should or should not consider changing the time students start lessons each morning.

In your letter you should:

- evaluate information on adolescents' sleep patterns
- give your views on changing the start of the school day
- discuss how the changes might affect parents and teachers.

Base your letter on what you have read in **Text A** but be careful to use your own words. Address all the bullet points.

Begin your letter: "Dear Principal, I have been reading about …"

Write about 250–350 words.

Up to 15 marks are available for the content of your answer, and up to 25 marks for the quality of your writing.

....

....

....

....

....

....

....

....

Exam tip

Don't forget to ...

- plan your composition around topic sentences that lead to an effective conclusion
- include details you annotated in the text in your plan before you start writing
- write in the appropriate style and a formal to neutral register
- clearly express your own thoughts and opinions in role
- check and correct your composition.

[40]

(If you need more lines, use an extra sheet of paper. Remember to write your name and the question number at the top.)

Activity

Section B: Composition

Answer one question from Section B.

Write about 350–450 words on **one** of the following questions.

Up to 16 marks are available for the content and structure of your answer, and up to 24 marks for the style and accuracy of your writing.

EITHER
Descriptive Writing

2 Describe a visit to a theme park, fairground or carnival.

OR
Descriptive Writing

3 Describe the last moments before you leave a place for ever.

OR
Narrative Writing

4 "Whispering". Use this as the title of a narrative.

OR
Narrative Writing

5 Write a story that starts with someone entering an old building or historic site.

Please write your chosen question number here (**2, 3, 4, 5**):

....

....

....

....

....

....

....

....

....

....

....

....

....

....

....

....

....

....

....

....

....

....

....

....

....

....

....

....

....

....

....

....

....

....

....

....

....

....

....

....

....

[40]

(If you need more lines, use an extra sheet of paper. Remember to write your name and the question number at the top.)

Apply

1 Read the marking guide for Paper 2 Section A on page 203, then mark your letter for its content, style and technical accuracy (spelling, punctuation, grammar).

Content	.... /15 marks
Style and accuracy	.... /25 marks
Total	.... /40 marks

2 Make notes in the table below on what you did well and how you could improve.

	What was done well	How I could improve
Content		
Style		
Accuracy		

3 Read the marking schemes for Paper 2 Section B on page 204, then mark your composition for its content, style and technical accuracy.

Content	.... /16 marks
Style and accuracy	.... /24 marks
Total	.... /40 marks

4 Make notes here on what you did well and how you could improve.

Content	My composition is interesting/convincing because …	
	My composition would be more interesting/convincing if I …	
Style	My writing style is affective and effective because I have used …	
	My writing style would be more affective and effective if I …	
Technical accuracy	Spelling	There are only …….. mistakes.
	Grammar	There are only …….. mistakes.
	Punctuation	There are only …….. mistakes.
	I can improve my marks for this if I …	

Raise your grade for Paper 2

Don't lose any marks!

- **Generally:** Make sure you read the questions properly and check your writing before you hand it in.
- **Reading for Question 1:**
  - Read the text(s) carefully. Underline ideas and annotate the texts *according to the task*.
  - Be sure to use ideas from the whole text or both texts in your answer.
  - Avoid repeating ideas or content directly; criticise or question what is in the text(s) *according to the task*.
  - Look for clues that the writer's or speaker's viewpoint may be biased.
  - Include and develop implicit ideas and evaluate more obvious content.
  - Use *all* the bullet points in your planning.
- **Writing for Question 1:**
  - Keyword the purpose, form and style (text type) for the task as you read the question. Use these in your plan and double-check them before you are halfway through your answer.
  - Organise your ideas before writing. Plan the structure of your response (paragraphing) carefully.
  - Tick off planned details as you write them in your answer.
  - Use words wisely and deliberately. Avoid repeating words, using a simple vocabulary or copying from the text(s).
  - Vary sentence structures. Stay in the correct tense. Use connecting words and phrases to link your ideas in paragraphs.
  - Remember the audience for your response. Don't forget the style and register for the task.

- **Writing for Questions 2–5:**
  - Choose a question that matches your strengths.
  - Plan before you write.
  - Decide on the end of a story before you begin.
  - Don't forget to start a new line for each new person speaking in dialogue.
  - Use interesting, original similes and metaphors.
  - Check every word in your composition before the end of the exam.

Review

Take a few minutes to review your thoughts about doing Paper 2.

How I felt about answering Question 1	
I can improve my marks for Question 1 (Section A) by …	
How I felt about writing my composition for Section B	
I can improve my marks for Section B by …	
Good ideas for Directed Writing:	

Good ideas for Narrative Writing:	
Good ideas for Descriptive Writing:	
What else I need to focus on to raise my grade in Paper 2:	
My target grade for Paper 2 is now …	

Objectives
In this unit you will:

- Practise answering exam-style papers under timed conditions.

Practice Paper 1 – Reading

Review

Before you tackle the sample Paper 1 in this unit, use the table below to list your thoughts about taking the exam. Research shows that students who identify what they feel concerned about and what they feel confident about before doing a test perform better than those who do not.

I feel concerned about …	I feel confident about …

In the exam, you will have 2 hours for Paper 1 and you need to use every minute for maximum marks.

When you start this sample paper, make a note of the time. Record how long it takes to read the texts (it should take 10–15 minutes), then how long it takes to read and answer each question.

As you do more practice papers, aim to complete your work in 2 hours. Make sure you leave sufficient time to go over your answers and correct any mistakes. You can take advantage of any extra time to answer any questions you didn't finish.

Practice paper 1 – reading

Paper 1 is compulsory

Instructions

- Answer all the questions.
- Use a black or dark blue pen.
- Write your answer to each question in the space provided.
- Do **not** use an erasable pen or correction fluid (cross out mistakes with a single line).
- If additional space is needed, use a piece of paper.
- Dictionaries are **not** allowed.

Information

- The total mark for this practice paper is 80.
- The number of marks for each question or part of question is shown in brackets [ ].

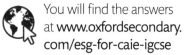
You will find the answers at www.oxfordsecondary.com/esg-for-caie-igcse

Text A: Scythian warriors

The following passage is a British Museum blog article by Chloe Leighton about the Scythians, a nomadic people who migrated westward from Central Asia to southern Russia and Ukraine in the 8th and 7th centuries BCE. The Scythians founded a powerful empire thanks to their domestication of wild horses.

Have you ever found yourself wondering who was the first person to decide to jump on a horse and ride it? It's a good chance that it was a Scythian!

The horse was an essential part of Scythian life and was the most important and multipurpose animal used by the nomads. Initially, the Scythians reared large herds of horses mainly for their milk and hides,
5   but eventually were among the first people to harness the horse as a mount. As you can imagine, this was a great success for the Scythians as it meant they could expand their horizons by moving at speeds of up to 30–40 miles an hour, they could push past environmental boundaries that immobilised those who travelled by foot, and their cavalry became the driving force behind their military might.

By the 7th century BC the Scythians were already master horsemen and controlled a vast corridor of
10 land that stretched across southern Siberia, from the Black Sea to the fringes of northern China. This expanse of land was greater than the Achaemenid Persian Empire, which the Scythians outlasted.

The Scythians also invented the earliest form of a saddle, arguably one of their biggest contributions to human civilisation. This invention spread like wildfire across their sedentary neighbours to the south and has stood the test of time. Over centuries, the Scythians kept perfecting their horse equipment,
15 which in turn meant they honed their horse riding skills.

But the Scythians did not stop there. They also invented an early version of a powerful composite bow that could discharge arrows at a considerably greater force and distance. They also designed the *gorytos*, a combined bow-case and quiver, that allowed a Scythian to carry his bow and arrows together for easier access whilst on horse-back. These revolutionary inventions meant that the
20 combination of a Scythian archer and his horse was a real *tour de force*.

[...] Anyone coming to the exhibition will be left in no doubt that horses were central to the Scythian way of life. Without them, it seems unlikely that the Scythians would have survived, let alone thrived and prospered for over 500 years.

https://blog.britishmuseum.org

Text B: An ancient polo match

The Ancient Greek form of polo, tzukanion, was played by teams of men and women on horseback using mallets made from bamboo poles. In this text the game is being played in 15th-century Trebizond, a city-state in what is now Turkey. A doctor named Tobie is watching.

It became apparent, before the major games were half over, that tzukanion played in the normal way between teams of powerful men was one of the noisiest games in existence. The players, once roused, roared, cursed and snarled in between trying to dislodge one another
5 from the saddle in order to improve their stroke. Hooves thundered, harness rattled. In case silence should fall, the stadium was surrounded by buglers and drummers. The drums set up a war beat that made the horses lay their ears back and roused the spectators to frenzy. The orders to end the phase, or the game, were conveyed by wild and elaborate
10 outbursts of trumpeting. Added to the continual roar of the crowd, it produced something very close to the sound of a pitched battle, which, Tobie thought, was probably the original idea. He was moderately surprised when the heavy games came to an end with only two horses dead and eight injured, and a few broken limbs here and there.

15 Attendants came on to the ground and raked and sprayed the dust till it caked and went dark. There was organ music, and some flutes, and a scattering of clowns came out and tumbled and threw dirt at one another […] Grooms bustled in behind the rails with strings of fresh ponies, and pages took off the broken sticks and, running back, resumed
20 their places all round the stadium with replacements held ready. The bamboo they were made of was whippy, and the mallet head was fixed to the end like a foot. In the stadium, they had repainted the gold lines at either end over which the ball had to be driven, to score points of credit. The ball was also bright gold.

25 The women's team, riding on first, was received by a modified silence, which represented, it would appear, the customary mark of respect. As was court practice, the noblewomen rode astride. […] In the left hand, each girl grasped a riding cane with her pony's reins wrapped round her fingers or over her elbow. In her right, the bamboo stood, slim and
30 straight […] The little, deep-chested horses paced under them; their cloth of gold burned and twinkled like armour, and it was hard to know which of them to look at.

From *The Spring of the Ram* by Dorothy Dunnett

Text C: A travel writer in the desert

 In this text a British journalist describes a visit to the Libyan desert in North Africa.

The plateau, the high dunes, the dry wadi beds and the verdant oases of the South Western desert are a veritable open air museum. The "Fezzan" is littered with millions of pre-historic
5 spear heads; arrow heads; crushing and cutting tools; shards of pottery; and even the eggshells of ostriches from pre-history. On my very first day, lunching in the shade of an acacia tree, I picked up a Stone Age cutting tool that was
10 literally lying at my feet.

Twelve thousand years of civilisation can be charted through the engravings and delicate rock paintings demonstrating the slow march of climate change – the shift from hunting to
15 pastoral pursuits; tribal differences; mysterious religious ceremonies; the introduction of the horse; and finally, as the desert encroached, the camel.

The talented artists who engraved their
20 observations in the rocky cliffs above the winding river beds had a purity of line of which Picasso would have been envious. I saw the gentle movements of giraffes, the lumbering bulk of rhino, the last moments of a dying elephant
25 and the lassoing of a group of ostriches.

As we wandered the desert we saw a camel giving birth; we ambled through wadis accompanied by chirping mulla mulla birds; we came across cracked, salt lakes where strange,
30 bulbous trees live and die; snowy white patches of gypsum; swathes of green plants with pale purple flowers (a consequence of only three days' rain two months before); we raced in 4x4s, our Tuareg drivers vying with each other to get
35 there first (wherever "there" was) and we leapt over impossible, impassable dunes whipped into geometric knife-edges by the ever-present desert wind; and unforgettably lazed beside the great blue-green slashes of still water, fringed with
40 succulent date palms and stands of pampas grass that comprise the beautiful oases where turtle doves flutter through the air, tiny pink shrimps swirl in the water and, on one occasion, a solitary white camel was tethered on the shady bank.

45 White camels are highly prized and our driver told me that his family had won races across the Arab world with his fifteen-strong herd. When I explained that England has no desert, he exclaimed sadly "then there is no yellow."
50 The Tuareg are not of Libya, Algeria, Niger, or Mali, they are the people of the Sahara. Proud, honest and exceedingly generous, they are a joy to be around. They acted as our drivers, guides and cooks, regaling us with traditional songs,
55 dispensing chilled water from goat skin bags, and on one occasion picking herbs from a desert bush to alleviate constipation! Every day after lunch they brewed Tuareg champagne – strong green tea boiled over a driftwood fire, poured
60 from a height to make cappuccino-like foam, then reheated and poured into small glasses with plenty of sugar. They seemed to genuinely enjoy showing us their territory. But they have had to adapt, choose a nationality, settle in villages and
65 learn Arabic, French, Italian and English.

The Tuareg were a thorn in the side of ancient Rome, plundering the trade routes from Africa to the port of Leptis Magna (one hour east of Tripoli). Eventually the Romans were forced to
70 make peace, to safeguard the vital shipments of ivory, slaves, and the thirty-five thousand wild animals that were sent to Rome for gladiatorial displays – graphically shown in Ridley Scott's box office smash *Gladiator*. The
75 decadent Emperor Commodus made Leptis Magna rich and one of its citizens, Septimus Severius, became Emperor of Rome. The remains of the city, with its theatre, temples, courts of justice, market, saunas, latrines, hunting baths,
80 and lighthouse were intact before the war.

The historical monuments, the pre-historic rock paintings, and the camaraderie of the fiercely loyal, intelligent and resourceful Tuareg people combined to make this my most highly prized
85 journey throughout the world. Not to mention the romance of the desert.

Adapted from an article by Angela Clarence, *The Observer* (21 May 2000)

📖 **Activity**

Read **Text A, *Scythian warriors*,** and then answer **Question 1(a)–(e).**

Question 1

(a) Give **two** examples of how the Scythians used horses before they became mounted warriors.

- ....

- ....

[1]

(b) Using your own words, explain what the text means by:

(i) "the first people to harness the horse as a mount" (line 5) ....

....

[2]

(ii) "it meant they could expand their horizons" (line 6) ....

....

[2]

(c) Re-read paragraph 4 ("The Scythians also invented ... riding skills.")
Give **two** reasons why the Scythians are famous for their connection to horses.

- ....

....

- ....

....

[2]

(d) Re-read paragraphs 5 and 6 ("But the Scythians did not stop ... over 500 years.")

(i) Identify **two** other revolutionary inventions of the time.

- ....

- ....

[2]

(ii) Explain why the writer says the Scythians "thrived and prospered for over 500 years." (lines 22–3)

....

....

....

[3]

(e) Re-read paragraphs 2 and 3 ("The horse was … the Scythians outlasted.")
Using your own words, explain how the Scythian "cavalry became the driving force
behind their military might".

....

....

....

[3]

Read **Text B, *An ancient polo match*,** and then answer **Question 1(f).**

Question 1

(f) According to **Text B**, what made tzukanion such an exciting and entertaining spectacle?
You must **use continuous writing** (not note form) and **use your own words** as far as possible.
Your summary should be no more than 120 words.
**Up to 10 marks are available for the content of your answer and up to 5 marks for the
quality of your writing.**

....

....

....

....

....

....

....

....

....

....

....

....

....

....

....

....

....

....

....

....

....

....

....

....

....

....

....

....

....

....

....

....

....

....

....

....

....

....

....

....

....

.... **[15]**

(If you need more lines, use an extra sheet of paper. Remember to write your name and the question number at the top.)

[Total: 30]

Read **Text C, *A travel writer in the desert*,** and then answer **Question 2(a)–(d).**

Question 2

(a) Identify a word or phrase from the text that suggests the same idea as the <u>words underlined</u>:

(i) Thousands of years of civilisation <u>can be traced</u> through rock paintings and climate change.

....

[1]

(ii) The <u>move from killing and eating wild animals to farming</u>.

....

[1]

(iii) The water, date palms and pampas grass that <u>make up</u> the oases.

....

[1]

(iv) Drivers were <u>competing</u> with each other.

....

[1]

(b) Using your own words, explain what the writer means by each of the words underlined:

The Tuareg were <u>a thorn in the side</u> of ancient Rome, <u>plundering</u> the trade routes from Africa to the port of Leptis Magna (one hour east of Tripoli). Eventually the Romans were forced to make peace. <u>To safeguard</u> the vital shipments of ivory, slaves, and the thirty-five thousand wild animals that were sent to Rome for gladiatorial displays graphically shown in Ridley Scott's box office smash *Gladiator*.

(i) a thorn in the side   ....   **[1]**

(ii) plundering   ....   **[1]**

(iii) To safeguard   ....   **[1]**

(c) Use **one** example from the text below to explain how the writer conveys her experiences and feelings about her trip to the desert in her article.

Use your own words in your explanation.

The historical monuments, the pre-historic rock paintings, and the camaraderie of the fiercely loyal, intelligent and resourceful Tuareg people combined to make this my most highly prized journey throughout the world. Not to mention the romance of the desert.

....

....

....

....

....

....

[3]

(d) Re-read paragraphs 4 and 5.

- Paragraph 4 begins, "As we wandered the desert ..." and is about the plants and dunes the writer sees.
- Paragraph 5 begins, "White camels are highly prized ..." and is about the Tuareg people of the Sahara.

Explain how the writer uses language to convey meaning and to create effect in these paragraphs. Choose **three** examples of words and phrases from **each** paragraph to support your answer. Your choices should include the use of imagery.

Write about 200–300 words.

Up to 15 marks are available for the content of your answer.

....

....

....

....

....

....

....

....

....

....

....

....

....

....

....

....

....

....

....

....

(d) Re-read paragraphs 4 and 5.

....

....

....

....

....

....

....

....

....

....

....

....

....

....

....

.... **[15]**

(If you need more lines, use an extra sheet of paper. Remember to write your name and the question number at the top.)

[Total: 25]

Re-read **Text C, *A travel writer in the desert*,** and then answer **Question 3.**

Question 3

Imagine you are a photographer who was with the writer of this travel article. On your return from the Libyan desert you are interviewed on a travel show about the trip. The interviewer asks you the following three questions only:

- What did you see **and** feel during your visit to the desert?
- What was your opinion of the people you were travelling with?
- Was this also your "most highly prized journey"?

Write the words of the interview.

Base your interview on what you have read in **Text C**, but be careful to use your own words. Address the three bullet points.

Begin your interview with the first question.

Write about 250–350 words.

Up to 15 marks are available for the content of your answer and up to 10 marks for the quality of your writing.

....

....

....

....

....

....

....

....

[25]

(If you need more lines, use an extra sheet of paper. Remember to write your name and the question number at the top.)

Review

Take a few minutes to review your thoughts about doing Paper 1.

I spent .... minutes reading the texts.
Question 1(a)–(e) took me a total of .... minutes.
Question 1(f) took me .... minutes.
Question 2(a)–(d) took me .... minutes.
Question 3 took me .... minutes.
I have improved most in the following questions:
I still have to improve these skills (note the question numbers too):
My own notes:

Practice Paper 2 – Directed Writing and Composition

 **Review**

Before you tackle Section A in this sample Paper 2, use the table below to write down your ideas on how you can gain more marks for your compositions – or not lose them.

Reading	Writing

In the exam, you will have 2 hours for Paper 2 and you need to use every minute for maximum marks.

When you start this sample paper, make a note of the time. Record how long it takes to read the text(s), then how long it takes to read and answer each question.

Try to complete your work in 2 hours. Make sure you leave sufficient time to go over your answers and correct any mistakes. You can take advantage of any extra time to proofread and correct punctuation.

Practice paper 2 directed writing and composition

Paper 2 is not compulsory: you may submit a Coursework Portfolio instead.

Instructions

- Answer **two** questions in total:
  Section A: answer **Question 1**.
  Section B: answer **one** question.
- Use a black or dark blue pen.
- Write your answer to each question in the space provided.
- Do **not** use an erasable pen or correction fluid (cross out mistakes with a single line).
- If additional space is needed, use a piece of paper.
- Dictionaries are **not** allowed.

Information

- The total mark for this exam-style paper is 80.
- The number of marks for each question or part of question is shown in brackets [ ].

Text A: The academic benefits of field trips

https://www.schooltripseducation.org

The following passage is an article on an educational website about the value of school trips and excursions.

Field trips, also known as school trips or excursions, offer students educational experiences out of the classroom and away from their regular school environment. Popular field trips include visits to nature reserves, fire stations, museums and local arts and crafts centres. Essentially, a field trip is a form of alternative education, providing students with an opportunity to experience something they might not

5   otherwise know about.

Students visiting professionally organised educational facilities out of school, such as purpose-built camps, can learn in a more hands-on and interactive manner than they would in school. Residential "school farms", for example, can provide primary age children with outdoor experiences such as picking crops, helping with milking or feeding chickens. Ordinary activities for our ancestors, but novelties for

10 most city-born children these days. In zoos, nature reserves and botanical gardens, young students can see live animals and plant life close up. At the other end of the age spectrum, engineering and science museums often have interactive displays that help older students to better understand the history of a discovery or industrial process.

Apart from the educational aspect, field trips provide a welcome break in routine. Students can look

15 forward to and prepare for the outing for days or weeks in advance, doing research in the library or online. They then spend time in a completely different learning environment, which brings a new understanding of the topic. Projects completed after a day trip will demonstrate a greater depth of understanding than those carried out entirely in the classroom. This is particularly valid and helpful for students who are more kinetic learners.

20 Field trips undertaken by older students can also expose them to a wide variety of professions or work environments, introducing them to job opportunities they might otherwise not have considered or even heard about.

In short, field trips can improve achievement in academic subjects in numerous ways. By experiencing first hand real-life applications of the lessons they are learning in school students come to understand

25 and appreciate topics more fully. They can also discover a new hobby or passion along the way.

Text B: Residential school trips

The following passage about school trips is taken from a daily newspaper.

As our society becomes increasingly risk-averse and litigious, we are in danger of suffocating our children in rules, regulations and cotton wool. Life is full of challenges
5   and we owe it to our children to equip them with the skills to recognise risks, assess them sensibly and react positively.

While it is possible to learn some basic concepts in class, there is no substitute for
10   real experience in the wider world. School trips provide a great opportunity for pupils to gain such experience and face a range of challenges that can contribute significantly to their personal development.

15   Pupils may feel that they know their classmates and teachers well from day-to-day contact in school, but the experience of living with them in a residential community can add a completely new
20   dimension. It raises the whole area of interpersonal skills, including leadership, team work and trust and respect.

There are also issues concerning the psychology of the whole experience,
25   particularly involving self-confidence, self-esteem and resilience. We frequently hear from teachers that pupils who do not normally shine in the classroom have excelled on a residential trip. This can all help to improve performance and relationships back at school.

School trips can also make a major contribution to the acquisition of knowledge and development of skills. Studies of the
30   natural and man-made world, the present and past, science and arts, language and music can all be enhanced outside the classroom. Adventure activity and sports skills can form the foundation of life-long
35   interests, as well as address the health and obesity agendas.

Of course, no mention of school trips can ignore the possibility of danger. While accidents are distressing, though, statistics
40   don't support the level of concern that exists. An average of two or three child deaths occur per annum on all types of school trip (out of an estimated ten million days of school visits), compared with 400 in
45   road traffic accidents and 200 in the home. Whilst care should always be taken, it is important to keep the fear of accidents in perspective.

Although there are still some doubting
50   voices, the benefits to pupils are so great and the risks so containable that the future of school trips should be assured. Giving in to risk aversion would be to deny our children life-changing, positive experiences and wonderful opportunities to learn.

From *The Guardian*, 9 September 2008

 **Activity**

Read **Text A** and **Text B** and then answer **Section A, Question 1.**

Section A: Directed Writing

Question 1

Imagine you are an IGCSE student in a school that is considering cancelling all school excursions and field trips because a group of students behaved badly during a recent trip and one of the students was injured. Your school principal says the money can be better spent on improving the school's library. You are a member of the school council.

Write a speech to be given during a council meeting, giving your views on the advantages of continuing with school field trips.

In your speech you should:

• evaluate the benefits and risks of field trips given in **both** texts
• give your views, based on what you have read, on how staff and students benefit from school trips.

Base your speech on what you have read in **both** texts but be careful to use your own words. Address both the bullet points.

Begin your speech: "Members of the school council, I would like to talk about …"

Write about 250–350 words.

Up to 15 marks are available for the content of your answer, and up to 25 marks for the quality of your writing.

....

....

....

....

....

....

....

....

....

....

....

....

....

....

....

....

....

[40]

(If you need more lines, use an extra sheet of paper. Remember to write your name and the question number at the top.)

Section B: Composition

Answer one question from Section B.

Write about 350–450 words on one of the following questions.

Up to 16 marks are available for the content and structure of your answer, and up to 24 marks for the style and accuracy of your writing.

EITHER

Descriptive Writing

2   Describe a celebration or party involving members of different age groups.

OR

Descriptive Writing

3   Describe a bus or railway journey.

OR

Narrative Writing

4   Write a story that includes the words "you have to believe me".

OR

Narrative Writing

5   Write a story in which someone makes a discovery.

Please write your chosen question number here (**2, 3, 4, 5**):

....

....

....

....

....

....

....

....

....

....

....

....

....   **[40]**

(If you need more lines, use an extra sheet of paper. Remember to write your name and the question number at the top.)

Review

Take a few minutes to review your thoughts about doing Paper 2.

Section A took me a total of .... minutes. I spent .... minutes reading the texts, ... minutes planning my answer and .... minutes editing and correcting my answer.

Section B took me .... minutes. I spent .... minutes planning my composition and .... minutes editing and correcting my answer.

In Section B, I chose Question .... because ...

This was a good/bad decision because ...

I still have to improve these skills (note the question numbers too):

My own notes:

In this section you will find basic marking guidelines for Papers 1 and 2 and Components 3 and 4.

Paper 1 – Reading

Question 1(a)–(e): Comprehension task

Marks depend on the content and nature of Text A.

Question 1(f): Summary task

Marks depend on the content and nature of Text B. You can, however, use the following marking guides to assess your general performance in this question.

Table A: Reading for Question 1(f) (up to 10 marks for content)

Level	Marks	
5	9–10	• A very effective response that shows thorough understanding of the task • Understands a wide range of relevant ideas; well-focused • Points are selected skilfully
4	7–8	• An effective response that shows competent understanding of the task • Understands of a good range of relevant ideas; mostly focused • Carefully selected points and some evidence of an overview
3	5–6	• A partially effective response that shows reasonable understanding of the task • Demonstrates basic understanding but occasional loss of focus • Relevant ideas selected but may include excess or unnecessary material
2	3–4	• A basic response that shows some understanding of the task • A general understanding of some ideas; sometimes focused • There may be some irrelevant or indiscriminate selection of ideas
1	1–2	• A response that shows limited understanding of the task • A basic list of unconnected ideas with limited focus • Limited evidence of selection

Table B: Writing for Question 1(f) (up to 5 marks for quality)

Level	Marks	
3	4–5	• A relevant response that is clear, fluent and concise • Well organised and structured • Uses own words (where appropriate); good range of well-chosen vocabulary to clarify meaning
2	2–3	• A relevant response that is generally clear, with some evidence of being concise • Some weaknesses in organisation • Mainly expressed in own words (where appropriate) but some reliance on words from the text
1	1	• A relevant response that is not clear or concise • Excessively long explanations or too brief • Sections lifted from the text

Question 2: Short-answer questions and Language task

Marks depend on the content and nature of Text C.

Question 3: Extended response to reading

Marks depend on the content and nature of Text C. You can, however, use the following marking guides to assess your general performance in this question.

Table A: Reading for Question 3 (up to 15 marks for content)

Level	Marks	
5	13–15	• A thorough evaluation and analysis of the text • Uses a wide range of relevant ideas, which are well developed, sustained and relate appropriately to the text • Well-selected supporting detail is integrated into the response, contributing to a strong sense of purpose and approach • Covers all bullet points well • Uses a consistent and convincing voice
4	10–12	• A competent reading of the text with evidence of basic evaluation or analysis • Uses a good range of ideas; some are developed but may not be sustained • Frequent relevant and helpful supporting detail contributing to a clear sense of purpose • Covers all bullet points • Uses an appropriate voice
3	7–9	• The text has been read reasonably well, understood and developed • Uses a range of straightforward ideas but opportunities for development are not exploited • Supporting detail is present but may include only basic use of the text • Uneven focus on the bullet points • The voice is plain, lacking in character
2	4–6	• A general understanding of the main ideas but may lack content and/or focus on the text or question • Brief, straightforward reference to the text • Over-reliance or lifting from the text • One of the bullet points may not be addressed • The voice may be inappropriate
1	1–3	• Little reference to the text or reproduction of sections from the text • Content is either insubstantial or unselective • Material from the text has not been modified or developed

Table B: Writing for Question 3 (up to 10 marks for quality (structure, order, style of language))

Level	Marks	
5	9–10	• Uses an effective register for the audience and purpose (task) • Uses language that sounds convincing and appropriate • Expresses ideas in a convincing manner using a wide range of effective and/or interesting language • Organisation, structure and sequence are sound throughout
4	7–8	• Some awareness of an appropriate register for audience and purpose • Mostly fluent use of English with clarity of expression • Sufficient range of vocabulary to express ideas with subtlety and precision • Organisation is well structured and well sequenced
3	5–6	• Language is clear but plain and/or factual, expressing little opinion • Ideas are rarely extended, but explanations are adequate • Some sections may be well sequenced but there may be flaws in the structure
2	3–4	• Some awkwardness of expression and/or style is inconsistent • Language is too limited to express shades of meaning • Some structural weaknesses and/or copying from the text
1	1–2	• Expression and structure lack clarity • Language is weak and undeveloped • Very little attempt to explain ideas • Frequent copying from the original

Paper 2 – Directed Writing and Composition

Section A: Directed Writing Question 1

Use the following marking guides to assess your general performance in this question.

Table A: Reading for Question 1 (up to 15 marks for content)

Level	Marks	
6	13–15	• Successfully evaluates ideas and opinions, both explicit and implicit • Assimilates ideas from the text to give a developed, sophisticated response
5	10–12	• Some successful evaluation of ideas and opinions, both explicit and implicit • A thorough response, supported by a detailed selection of relevant ideas from the text
4	7–9	• Begins to evaluate mainly explicit ideas and opinions • An appropriate response that includes relevant ideas from the text
3	5–6	• Selects and comments on explicit ideas and opinions • Makes a general response including a few relevant ideas from the text
2	3–4	• Identifies explicit ideas and opinions • Makes a limited response with little evidence from the text
1	1–2	• Very limited response with minimal relation to the text

Table B: Writing for Question 1 (up to 25 marks for quality)

Level	Marks	
6	22–25	• A very effective style capable of conveying subtle meaning • Carefully structured paragraphs for benefit of the reader • A wide range of sophisticated vocabulary, used precisely • An effective register for audience and purpose (style) • Spelling, punctuation and grammar are almost always accurate
5	18–21	• An effective, appropriate style • Good overall structure, organised to help the reader reach a conclusion • A wide range of vocabulary, used with some precision for effect • An appropriate register for audience and purpose of composition • Spelling, punctuation and grammar are mostly accurate with only occasional minor errors
4	14–17	• Sometimes effective style but not always consistent • Ideas are generally well sequenced in clear paragraphs • Vocabulary is adequate and sometimes effective • Register is generally appropriate for audience and purpose • Spelling, punctuation and grammar are generally accurate, but include some errors
3	10–13	• Style is inconsistent and use of English awkward but meaning is generally clear • Composition follows same sequence as the original text • Vocabulary is simple and limited, and/or relies on the original text • Some awareness of an appropriate register for audience and purpose • Frequent spelling mistakes; punctuation and grammar are poor
2	6–9	• Style is very limited • Paragraphs are not well organised or in a sequence • Vocabulary is very limited and/or relies on the original text • Little awareness of appropriate register for audience and purpose • Persistent spelling, punctuation and grammar mistakes
1	1–5	• Expression is unclear and hard to understand • Very poor organisation or sequencing of ideas • Very limited vocabulary or copied from the original text • Inappropriate register (or no register) for audience and purpose • Persistent errors in spelling, punctuation and grammar make composition hard to read and understand

Marking guidelines

Section B: Composition Questions 2–5

Use the following marking guides to assess your general performance in these questions.

Table A: Content for Questions 2–5 (up to 16 marks for content and structure)

Level	Marks	Content and structure
6	14–16	• An engaging and effective composition, complex and structured carefully for a deliberate effect • **Descriptive composition:** Well-defined ideas and images; uses sensory imagery and figurative language with variety of focus • **Narrative composition:** Storyline is clear and developed using fiction writing techniques such as characterisation, description, rising action and climax, with convincing original details
5	11–13	• Engaging and effective content with well-developed and engaging structure for a deliberate effect • **Descriptive composition:** Carefully selected and presented images and details to create a mostly convincing scene or occasion • **Narrative composition:** Storyline developed using fiction writing techniques such as characterisation, description and climax, with convincing details
4	8–10	• Content is relevant to the question with some development; structure is clear for effect • **Descriptive composition:** Includes a selection of relevant ideas and images but style and structure is narrative • **Narrative composition:** Relevant storyline and cohesive paragraphing; uses some fiction techniques such as setting and characterisation
3	5–7	• Straightforward response to the question, limited development and structure, which may not always be effective • **Descriptive composition:** Question is answered but in a narrative style with few descriptive elements • **Narrative composition:** Plot is straightforward but content is not effective; some attempt to use fiction writing techniques
2	3–4	• Content is very simple or basic; structure lacks organisation and has limited effect • **Descriptive composition:** An account that includes some relevant details but is not always consistent or in accord with the question • **Narrative composition:** Very simple plot with events that are not presented clearly or for an effect
1	1–2	• Content is only partially relevant or clear; ineffective structure • **Descriptive composition:** Description lacks clarity and relevant details • **Narrative composition:** Storyline is undeveloped and/or lacks coherence

Table B: Writing for Questions 2–5 (up to 24 marks for style and accuracy)

Level	Marks	Style and accuracy
6	21–24	• Well-chosen and precise vocabulary • Varied sentence structures chosen for effect • Register entirely suitable for the context • Spelling, punctuation and grammar accurate with only minor mistakes; evidence of careful proofreading
5	17–20	• Mostly precise vocabulary • A range of sentence structures used effectively • Mainly consistent and appropriate register for the context • Spelling, punctuation and grammar mostly accurate, with only occasional minor errors
4	13–16	• Some precise vocabulary • A range of sentence structures, some used for deliberate effect • Generally appropriate register for the context • Spelling, punctuation and grammar generally accurate, but with some errors
3	9–12	• Simple and basic vocabulary • Limited use of sentence structures • Simple register for the context • Frequent spelling, punctuation and grammar errors, occasionally serious
2	5–8	• Limited and/or imprecise vocabulary • Limited sentence structures • Limited and/or inappropriate register for context • Persistent spelling, punctuation and grammar mistakes
1	1–4	• Imprecise and/or incorrect vocabulary and sentence structures • Register demonstrates little or no sense of the context • Persistent spelling, punctuation and grammar mistakes which make reading difficult

Component 3 – Coursework Portfolio

Assignment 1

Use the following marking guides to assess your general performance in this assignment.

Table A: Reading for Assignment 1 (up to 15 marks)

Level	Marks	
6	13–15	• Successfully evaluates explicit and implicit ideas and opinions • Assimilates ideas from the text to give a developed, sophisticated response
5	10–12	• Some successful evaluation of ideas and opinions, both explicit and implicit • A thorough response, supported by a detailed selection of relevant points from the text
4	7–9	• Begins to evaluate mainly explicit ideas and opinions • An appropriate response that includes relevant ideas from the text
3	5–6	• Selects and comments on explicit ideas and opinions • Makes a general response, including a few relevant ideas from the text
2	3–4	• Identifies explicit ideas and opinions • Makes a limited response with little evidence from the text
1	1–2	• Very limited response with minimal relation to the text

Table B: Writing for Assignment 1 (up to 15 marks)

Level	Marks	
6	13–15	• Highly effective style conveying subtle meaning • Carefully structured for the benefit of the reader • Wide range of sophisticated vocabulary used precisely for effect • Highly effective register for audience and purpose • Spelling, punctuation and grammar almost always accurate
5	10–12	• Effective style • Secure overall structure, organised to help the reader • Wide range of vocabulary, used with some precision • Effective register for audience and purpose • Spelling, punctuation and grammar mostly accurate with only minor errors
4	7–9	• Effective but inconsistent style • Ideas are mostly well sequenced • Vocabulary is adequate and sometimes effective • Mainly effective register for audience and purpose • Spelling, punctuation and grammar are generally accurate but include some errors
3	5–6	• Inconsistent style; expression sometimes awkward but meaning clear • Over-reliance on the sequence of the original text • Vocabulary is simple, limited or reliant on the original text • Some awareness of an appropriate register for audience and purpose • Frequent errors of spelling, punctuation and grammar, sometimes serious
2	3–4	• Limited style • Response is not well sequenced or structured • Limited vocabulary or words/phrases copied from the original text • Limited awareness of register for audience and purpose • Persistent errors of spelling, punctuation and grammar
1	1–2	• Expression unclear • Poor sequencing of ideas • Very limited vocabulary or copying from the original text • Very limited awareness of register for audience and purpose • Persistent spelling, punctuation and grammar errors hinder communication

Assignments 2 and 3

Use the following marking guides to assess your general performance in these assignments.

Table A: Content for Assignments 2 and 3 (up to 10 marks for content and structure in each assignment)

Level	Marks	
6	9–10	• Content is complex, engaging and effective • Structure is secure, well balanced and carefully managed for deliberate effect • **Assignment 2:** Many well-defined and developed ideas and images create a convincing overall picture with varieties of focus • **Assignment 3:** The plot is well defined and strongly developed with features of fiction writing such as description, characterisation and effective climax, and convincing details
5	7–8	• Content is developed, engaging and effective • Structure is well managed, with some choices made for deliberate effect • **Assignment 2:** Frequent, well-chosen images and details give a mostly convincing picture • **Assignment 3:** The plot is defined and developed with features of fiction writing such as description, characterisation, climax and details
4	5–6	• Content is relevant with some development • Structure is competently managed/organised • **Assignment 2:** A selection of relevant ideas, images and details, even where there is a tendency to write in a narrative style • **Assignment 3:** The plot is relevant and cohesive, with some features such as characterisation and setting of scene
3	3–4	• Content is straightforward and only briefly developed • Structure is mostly organised but may not always be effective • **Assignment 2:** The task is addressed with a series of relevant but straightforward details, which may be more typical of a narrative • **Assignment 3:** The plot is straightforward, with limited use of the features of narrative writing
2	2	• Content is simple, and ideas and events may be limited • Structure is partially organised but limited in its effect • **Assignment 2:** The recording of some relevant events with limited detail • **Assignment 3:** The plot is a simple story narrative that may consist of events that are only partially linked and/or which are presented with partial clarity
1	1	• Content is occasionally relevant or clear • Structure is limited, lacking focus and/or is ineffective • **Assignment 1:** The description is unclear and lacks detail • **Assignment 2:** The plot and/or narrative lack coherence

Table B: Writing for Assignments 2 and 3 (up to 15 marks for style and accuracy in each assignment)

Level	Marks	
6	13–15	• Precise, well-chosen vocabulary and varied sentence structures, chosen for effect • Consistent well-chosen register suitable for the context • Spelling, punctuation and grammar almost always accurate
5	10–12	• Mostly precise vocabulary with a range of sentence structures mostly for effect • Mostly consistent appropriate register suitable for the context • Spelling, punctuation and grammar mostly accurate, with occasional minor errors
4	7–9	• Some precise vocabulary with a range of sentence structures sometimes used for effect • Some appropriate register for the context • Spelling, punctuation and grammar generally accurate, but with some errors
3	5–6	• Simple vocabulary and a range of straightforward sentence structures • Simple register with a general awareness of the context • Frequent errors of spelling, punctuation and grammar, occasionally serious
2	3–4	• Limited and/or imprecise vocabulary and sentence structures • Limited and/or imprecise register for the context • Persistent errors of spelling, punctuation and grammar
1	1–2	• Frequently imprecise vocabulary and sentence structures • Register demonstrates little or no sense of the context • Persistent spelling, punctuation and grammar errors hinder communication

Component 4 – Speaking and Listening Test

Part 1: Individual talk

Use the following marking guides to assess your general performance in this talk.

Table A: Individual talk (up to 20 marks)

Level	Marks	
5	17–20	• Full control of the subject and well-organised use of content • Lively, engaging delivery • Uses a wide range of language devices (e.g. tone, irony, emphasis) accurately and with some eloquence • Appropriate and accurate use of language maintained throughout
4	13–16	• Good, competent use of content • Occasional hesitations but tries to engage the listener • Uses a good range of language devices (e.g. tone, irony, emphasis) • Mainly appropriate and accurate use of language
3	9–12	• Adequate use of content • Delivery is secure but at times unimaginative; some attempt to engage listener • Language devices (e.g. tone, irony, emphasis) are used appropriately • Aware of appropriate and accurate use of language, but some inaccuracy present
2	5–8	• Content is thin or talk lacks cohesion or flow; includes inconsistencies • Insecure delivery with little attempt to engage the listener • Limited use of language devices (e.g. tone, irony, emphasis) and with inaccuracies • Some appropriate use of language but with some inaccuracy
1	1–4	• Content is mostly undeveloped and/or very thin • Delivery is weak, with no attempt to engage the listener • Unable to use language devices (e.g. tone, irony, emphasis) or with serious error • Language is not used appropriately or is used with serious inaccuracy

Part 2: Conversation

Use the following marking guides to assess your general performance in this conversation. There are separate marks for speaking and for listening.

Table B: Speaking in Conversation (up to 10 marks)

Level	Marks	
5	9–10	• Extends the subject matter and elicits responses from the listener; speaks on equal terms with the listener • Employs a wide range of language devices (e.g. tone, irony, emphasis) accurately and sometimes eloquently; appropriate and accurate use of language maintained throughout
4	7–8	• Subject matter is organised and expressed competently; tries to speak on equal terms with the listener but with limited success • Employs a good range of language devices (e.g. tone, irony, emphasis); mainly appropriate and accurate use of language
3	5–6	• Deals with the subject matter in an adequate manner; the listener is generally but not always prominent • Language devices (e.g. tone, irony, emphasis) are used appropriately with accurate use of language, although some inaccuracy may be present
2	3–4	• There is evidence of some linking together of ideas relating to the subject matter but it is inconsistent; accepts that the listener is in full control of the conversation • Limited use of language devices (e.g. tone, irony, emphasis) with some inaccuracy; some appropriate use of language but with some inaccuracy
1	1–2	• Simple facts and ideas with little evidence of linking them; very little success as a two-way conversation • No use of language devices or devices (e.g. tone, irony, emphasis) used with serious error; no appropriate use of language or used with serious inaccuracy

Table B: Listening in Conversation (up to 10 marks)

Level	Marks	
5	9–10	• Natural and fluent conversation • Responds fully to questions and develops prompts; deals confidently and sometimes enthusiastically with new direction(s) of conversation
4	7–8	• Conversation is occasionally fluent and sometimes shaped by the candidate • Responds appropriately and in extended detail to questions and prompts; deals appropriately with most changes in direction of conversation
3	5–6	• Conversation is maintained through the candidate's responses • Responds to questions adequately; less effective with prompts; new direction or changes in direction of conversation occasionally dealt with
2	3–4	• Conversation is driven by the listener's questions • Provides limited response to questions and struggles to develop prompts; tends to maintain the direction of conversation
1	1–2	• Conversation is not maintained • Responds simply and no response to questions or prompts; no recognition of changes in direction of conversation